TRANSCENDING
TRAUMA

TRANSCENDING
TRAUMA

A GUIDE TO POST-TRAUMATIC GROWTH

BETH REECE

Paulist Press
New York / Mahwah, NJ

Artwork: p. 31, "The 'Stages of Grief'" by Cecilia Yang, www.theimaginarylibrary.com; p. 36, photograph, "#inthistogether" by Beth Reece; p. 61, "Transition," graph adapted by Beth Reece from William Bridges, *Transitions: Making Sense of Life's Changes* (Cambridge, MA: De Capo, 2004), and Sabina Spencer and John Adams, *Life Changes: A Guide to the Seven Stages of Personal Growth* (New York: Paraview, 2002); p. 85, "Post-Traumatic Growth Tools at Work..." by Beth Reece; p. 91, "Tree" by Meskalero, www.deviantart.com; p. 92, Circle of Support drawing by James R. Zullo, PhD; p. 109, "Laberinto 1" by Nordisk familjebok, Wikimedia Commons.

Cover image of tree graphic by Terranaut / Pixabay.com
Cover design by Joe Gallagher
Book design by Lynn Else

Library of Congress Cataloging-in-Publication Data
Names: Reece, Beth, author.
Title: Transcending trauma: a guide to post-traumatic growth / Beth Reece.
Description: New York; Mahwah, NJ: Paulist Press, 2024. | Summary: "This book explains the journey through trauma with its loss, grief, transition, and an application of post-traumatic tools for healing"—Provided by publisher.
Identifiers: LCCN 2024001806 (print) | LCCN 2024001807 (ebook) | ISBN 9780809157020 (paperback) | ISBN 9780809188727 (ebook)
Subjects: LCSH: Post-traumatic stress disorder—Religious aspects—Christianity. | Post-traumatic stress disorder—Religious aspects. | Pastoral psychology. | Post-traumatic growth.
Classification: LCC BV4910.45 .R44 2024 (print) | LCC BV4910.45 (ebook) | DDC 248.8/625—dc23/eng/20240711
LC record available at https://lccn.loc.gov/2024001806
LC ebook record available at https://lccn.loc.gov/2024001807

ISBN 978-0-8091-5702-0 (paperback)
ISBN 978-0-8091-8872-7 (ebook)

Published by Paulist Press
997 Macarthur Boulevard
Mahwah, New Jersey 07430
www.paulistpress.com

Printed and bound in the
United States of America

Dedication

"...knowing that suffering produces endurance, and endurance produces character, and character produces hope, and hope does not disappoint us, ..."

Romans 5:3–5 NRSVCE

Thank you to the staff and patients
of the Shirley Ryan AbilityLab
for teaching me that in community
healing and transcendence are possible.

CONTENTS

CONTENTS

ACKNOWLEDGMENTS

> "When one door closes, another opens; but we often look so long and so regretfully upon the closed door that we do not see the one which has opened for us."
>
> Alexander Graham Bell

Stopped in my tracks by work and family responsibilities from pursuing a DMin degree to investigate spiritual healing after trauma, Stephen Krupa, SJ, my spiritual director, opened the door to the idea of an independent study through Loyola. Many thanks to Jean-Pierre Fortin, PhD, and Therese Lysaught, PhD, who accepted the challenge, and enthusiastically suggested resources, comprehensive editing, encouragement, and pushed me to write about what I was learning. Therese has continued to offer support and faithfully checked on my progress all along the way. She also provided the connection to CMMB and Marcia Grand Ortega, manager of their volunteer program, who invited me to field test these concepts with their healthcare staffs in cross-cultural settings during COVID and encouraged continuing connection with the Eswatini Palliative Care Team.

Thanks to Jeanne Wirpsa, MA, BCC, HEC-C, program director of Medical Ethics at Northwestern Memorial Hospital, who first mentioned the concept of "Post Traumatic Growth," and provided helpful editing as well. Thanks to Michael Washington, MA, MDiv, PhD, and ACPE Certified Educator at Northwestern Memorial Hospital for his editorial comments that widened my understanding about cultural considerations of trauma, grief, and growth.

Thanks to all my communities: chaplain colleagues, peer group, Spiritual Care Team at Shirley Ryan AbilityLab, church group, friends, and family who listened to my story, patiently and persistently checked on my progress, and celebrated my discoveries.

Thanks to Paulist Press, Paul McMahon, Editorial Director; Trace Murphy, Editor-at-Large; and their team for choosing to publish and provide invaluable, thoughtful, editorial advice and guidance.

And thanks be to God, who has put into creation an abundance of tools for healing our suffering world.

INTRODUCTION

I write as a chaplain to other chaplains and to those who are caregivers for individuals or communities suffering from trauma. The experiences I describe come from my own patient encounters. This book is not about my life journey. But as I look back on trauma in my own life, I see how the tools described in this book impacted me and allowed me to find identity and purpose for a new life dedicated to loving others. This book isn't a "how-to" book for new chaplains either. Rather, it is about ways we can introduce a medically researched pattern of care that aligns with basic tenets of religious faith for a way up and out of trauma. It's about how our Spiritual Care Department at the Shirley Ryan AbilityLab applied this knowledge to patients, families, and staff at our hospital. This archetypal journey toward healing is certainly not limited to the healthcare environment. There is relevance for *any* individual, group, community, or town visited by trauma.

My background is in Christian spirituality. Basic to my tradition of faith is that suffering and struggle are part of life. Through these experiences, new life and transcendence are possible and often take us to new higher ground. Jesus is the prime example. His life has totally informed my work as a chaplain. I have carefully studied the way he approached people, the questions he asked, the conversations he invited. I have reflected on his own transformational journey through trauma. His death, resurrection, and new life provides example and brings salvation and hope. Seventeen years of listening to others' stories has taken me deeper into my own meaning making and practice of faith and experience of

God at work in all things. However, these tools for recovery apply to any religious background or spirituality because they minister deeply to our basic human needs of being loved; finding purpose, meaning, and identity; and surviving the traumas and challenges life throws at all of us.

Chaplaincy was an unplanned career for me later in life. Several of my own traumas caused me to reevaluate a twenty-year commodity brokerage business and to reflect on whether I was fully leaning into the true purpose of my life. My conclusion was that it was time for change. A two-year course in spiritual direction further affirmed a new path. I didn't know that those first steps out of commodity brokerage would end in chaplaincy. My spiritual director encouraged me that "God wastes nothing." Everything I had learned in my life would come to bear in whatever was next. A course in clinical pastoral education at Northwestern Hospital opened up the potential of chaplaincy for me. In 2004 I was hired by the Shirley Ryan AbilityLab, the leading hospital in physical rehabilitation. Our patient population comes from all over the world and represents a broad range of religious backgrounds and spirituality.

Advocacy for my customers transferred to advocacy for my patients. Patient and staff conversations often dived deep into the basic questions of the meaning of life. The challenge for me and our staff was to be as cutting edge in our spiritual care as the physical care offered by our outstanding translational research hospital. From that challenge came the answers written about in this book.

1

SEARCHING FOR ANSWERS

Sitting across from me was a patient about to be discharged from our hospital. His legs had been amputated due to complications with diabetes. We were in the midst of a ritual and blessing for limb loss. I asked if he had anything to share. And he nodded.

"Yes, I do. Being here has been a good experience," he began slowly. "The staff, the therapists have all helped me a lot. But they don't understand when I say that this [gestures at his missing legs] is the best thing that ever happened to me."

"Why do you say that?" I asked.

"Because I go home with a greater gratitude for my family and friends. I have survived! I feel that God has purpose for me. My faith has grown. I have a new appreciation for life, and I'm a better person than I was before this happened to me."

What was it that brought transformation and transcendence to this man, despite a permanent physical injury that many would consider horrific? Regardless of physical trauma or permanent bodily injury, spiritual and emotional healing is possible. I had experienced this kind of healing in my own life. After hearing his testimony, I wondered...How could I, a spiritual caregiver, help facilitate growth and change like this for *more* of our patients?

It was obvious to me that physical trauma has enormous if often ignored spiritual implications. What kind of holistic response might incorporate care to all aspects of our humanity? To quote Plato: "If the head and body are to be well, you must begin by curing the soul. That is the first thing." If the soul is our spiritual essence, then our spirit is the way we connect with what is beyond ourselves. "We all have a spirituality...whether we are religious or not,"[1] asserts Ronald Rolheiser. Our spirits channel and shape our desires, and choose our disciplines and habits. Our spirits give energy for life, with the possibilities of disintegration or integration. Trauma can deeply wound us by causing a loss of energy and identity. Is it true that if our physical situation improves, our spirit may begin to heal as well? If we are forced to relinquish previously held physical patterns and goals for life, can we still find a way to acceptance and meaning? I planned to review the relevant landscape of research and literature and hoped to find answers to my questions.

This seemed like a perfect opportunity for a DMin study project. But work and family responsibilities made this impossible. Upon the counsel of my spiritual director, Fr. Stephen Krupa, I embarked on a two-year study as an alternative, guided by two professors from the Institute of Pastoral Studies of Loyola University, Chicago: Therese Lysaught, PhD, and Jean-Pierre Fortin, PhD.

I found that others had been exploring the same questions, particularly psychologists, philosophers, and spiritual writers. In his excellent book *Upside*, Jim Rendon details the process of discovery. In the 1980s two psychology professors from the University of North Carolina, Richard Tedeschi and Lawrence Calhoun, began asking: "How can trauma upend everything someone knows about himself and force him to build a life and new and larger sense of self? How can someone come out on the other side of a terrible event better, wiser, and more fulfilled?"[2]

As Tedeschi and Calhoun interviewed people and searched for answers, they discovered that redemption, resilience, and more were indeed possible after severe trauma. "They began to see that traumatic experiences certainly did cause suffering, but suffering was not the end of the change wrought by these events. Suffering, in fact, was part of a much larger experience. It proved to be a kind of catalyst that pushed people to find new meaning in their lives."[3]

They likened it to the rebuilding that can come after an earthquake. The earthquake happens unexpectedly and is devastating. The rebuilding and adjustment are the growth, and a new, better, more resilient building gets constructed. They labeled this possibility for positive change as "post-traumatic growth" (PTG), which can occur following many kinds of traumas. It is both process and outcome. They interviewed people all over the world, and their research targeted all kinds of traumatic situations like car crashes, hurricanes, assaults, illnesses, and life events. As Tedeschi and Calhoun continued to dig, they eventually found positive change was occurring in five areas:

1. Increased inner strength.
2. An openness to new possibilities in life.
3. Closer and often deeper relationships with friends and family.
4. An enhanced appreciation for life.
5. A stronger sense of spirituality.[4]

They admit that it takes a seismic event—one that shakes you to your core—to ignite growth that results in new thinking, new assessment of self and world, and often better life than you had before the trauma. Recovery can begin quickly or take years. It can lead to major changes in your sense of self, your relationships, and your life philosophy/priorities. Their research showed that even severe levels of post-traumatic stress disorder (PTSD) might be redeemed.

"Growth as a result of trauma is more common than PTSD." In fact, Tedeschi says:

> PTSD often sets the stage for the kind of suffering and reassessment that is often required for growth. When a person is suffering from the symptoms of PTSD, that is the point at which he is beginning to try to make sense of the trauma, integrating his experience back into his everyday life and trying to rebuild his sense of self.[5]

That suffering makes us stronger is not a new concept. Archetypal myths of heroic journeys beginning with trauma and death run through all cultures and religions.

> From our oldest heroic myths to the stories of the lives of sacred religious figures to superheroes in blockbuster movies like Batman, who watched as his parents were murdered and dedicated his life to battling crime, we learn over and over that traumatic events have the power to transform us into better people and make our lives more meaningful.[6]

Even nature mirrors the story of achieving new life and death in the change of seasons, the chick's struggle to peck its way out of the egg, or the caterpillar's transformation to a butterfly. The idea that great good can come from great suffering is timeless. People *do* recover from trauma. But how? *How* does it happen?

The search to explore and explain has continued over centuries. Plato philosophized about the struggle that leads a person to new light and truth. Aristotle, in the fourth century BC, wrote about seemingly hopeless and helpless situations and proposed the concept of *eudaimonia*, that inherent drive within us for human flourishing and to find meaning, purpose, balance, and happiness. He observed the unique potential of humans driven to pursue the "best version of ourselves."

In the twentieth century, Viktor Frankl, a survivor of the Holocaust, founded an entire branch of psychotherapy called *logotherapy*, based on how we find meaning, make sense of suffering, and move through and forward to achieve a healthy life. He observed, "The way in which a man accepts his fate and all the suffering it entails, the way in which he takes up his cross, gives him ample opportunity—even under the most difficult circumstances—to add a deeper meaning to his life."[7] And he adds, "Even the helpless victim of a hopeless situation, facing a fate he cannot change, may rise above himself, may grow beyond himself, and by so doing change himself."[8]

Abraham Maslow, an American psychologist, published a paper in the 1940s, which took Aristotle's idea of human flourishing, in spite of suffering, to a deeper level. He laid out his concept of the hierarchy of needs: a pyramid with physiological needs at the base, next a layer of safety, then love, and lastly esteem at the top. Maslow's brilliant insight was that when these needs are met, self-actualization can occur. Its potential is built into us. We are made to seek what we lack and made to mend when we find it. Our bodies want to be well. Maslow defines self-actualization as "the full use and exploitation of talents, capacities, and potentialities. It echoes Friedrich Nietzsche's exhortation, 'Become what thou art!'"[9]

He found that among successful leaders, their most important learning experiences were often the tragedies and traumas that forced them to adopt a new perspective on their lives: "I think of the self-actualizing man not as an ordinary man with something added, but rather as the ordinary man with nothing taken away."[10] Recovery and more is possible. Not necessarily recovery as return to what was before but recovery maybe and even toward new higher ground, bigger, wider, deeper than previously experienced.

Stephen Joseph, Martin Seligman, and other psychologists have continued to add to research confirming that out of the ashes of trauma and suffering comes the possibility for new life, new purpose, new connectedness. The positive psychology movement developed by Seligman postulated a theory of well-being that names twenty-four character strengths that are pathways to positive emotions, engagement, relationships, meaning, and achievement.[11]

This shift in the environmental, social, psychological, and cultural determinants of health now asserts that "spiritual needs are a core health concept."[12] Hospitals formerly concentrated on disease prevention, but a new focus is on well-being. "Taking patients' spiritual needs into account is an integral component that directly facilitates positive health outcomes."[13] Understanding that spirituality plays a role has also contributed to a broader idea of its definition and requirements. Researchers identify spiritual needs of hospital patients: (1) meaning, purpose, and hope; (2) relationship with God; (3) spiritual practices; (4) religious obligations; (5) interpersonal connection; and (6) professional staff interactions. Whatever your ministry, these needs are going to be present for the people in your care.

This is where Tedeschi and Calhoun's research on post-traumatic growth has made a significant contribution. Exploring the concept of growth not only through adversity but also, as noted earlier, in interviews with trauma survivors worldwide, they have opened a pathway for healing and transformation. They cite the importance of sharing negative emotions, cognitive processing or rumination, and finding positive coping strategies. PTG can't cure the systemic racism, poverty, and violence that seems rampant in our culture. However, even as these communal challenges remain, research shows that the framework and application of these tools can support the human spirit, forge a way for emotional and spiritual healing, and enable survival despite our existence amid ongoing trauma that often finds its source in societal evils. From their work, tools have emerged that we can use to encourage spiritual healing and growth. They are:

- Story
- Community
- Hope
- Creativity
- Faith

Story, crafting our "narrative identity"[14] and telling the truth about our experience, is the first tool. Perhaps the most difficult. Sometimes trauma is so devastating that words seem insufficient and unreachable. It takes time to piece together in a bearable way the description and timeline of what happened. Even connecting to the past story or inserting it into the present can be challenging. Telling the full truth about damage received is a slow and painful process. The new reality is not only hard to bear but may also seem impossible to accept. Trauma changes us in ways that are only discoverable over time.

Putting words to your story is one thing. Who will hear it? Who will listen nonjudgmentally, compassionately, and patiently as you make your way through your experience? The next tool, **community**, provides space to find meaning and support, to be held with compassion, and to share your experience. We all need many "communities" for recovery. As trauma theory pioneer Bessel van der Kolk writes:

> Social support is the most powerful protection against becoming overwhelmed by stress and trauma. This is not the same as merely being in the presence of others. The critical issue is *reciprocity*: being truly heard and seen by the people around us, feeling that we are held in someone else's mind and heart.[15]

The virtue of truth is key for the first tool, and for the second, surrender is vital. It is in your openness to receive love, accept counsel and accountability, and acknowledgment that you can't do life alone, that the full benefits of community are effective.

Being held with compassion by others brings the courage and possibility for **hope**. Different from optimism, which is a positive thought pattern, hope reaches into the future for something real and true that moves one forward instead of backward, sets goals, and makes plans. Hope arrives in many ways: physical improvements, emotional stabilization, a returning sense of gratefulness, or enhanced spirituality. An emotion, tool, skill, and virtue, hope allows you to access experiences and memories that support meaning-making. It "can powerfully influence cognition and deliberative thinking...and impacts the machinery of perception, the circuits that are used to take in and process data and make decisions."[16] Hope received from sharing and caring with others gives strength for innovative thinking.

Creativity, tool number four, engenders in us curiosity, observation, appreciation, and imagination for what can be. Creativity allows us to count the disability but envision a future, to see possibilities and imagine solutions. Anthropologist Agustin Fuentes says, "Creativity is as much a part of our tool kit as walking on two legs and having a big brain."[17] Repressed by trauma, released by story, encouraged by community, and fostered through hope, this innovative thinking ignites an *openness to change*, necessary for forward movement. Empowerment comes from efficacy and choice. Creativity can be invited in all kinds of ways, through practice of mindfulness, prayer, journaling, art, music, nature, or body/mind exercises. The possibilities are endless.

Out of all this comes a new understanding and practice of **faith**. Those who hold a religious faith can find a powerful source for meaning and meaning-making in relation to a God who suffered and suffers with us still, and who finds new life in and through that suffering. For those who don't identify as religious, or would term themselves "spiritual," it opens the invitation to realize strength accessible beyond themselves. This new, deeper faith, born out of suffering, informs and enlarges the existing story, to place it within God's larger story, offering transcendence, new meaning, new purpose. Fresh wisdom adds hope and openness to a now deeper spiritual life. It is like an ascending, expanding spiral of connection and relatedness to others and to God. Not that this kind of spiritual formation isn't possible for all of us as we travel through life, but somehow, out of suffering and trauma, there is gift and impetus that can take us more deeply along this journey. Now we have a bigger story to tell about our transformation, which encompasses the ways we live and die, let go, begin again, choose, receive, and grow.

Any of us can appropriate these tools for trauma recovery. But it takes *all* the tools for the greatest recovery. Chaplains certainly can apply and expand on *all* these tools as they care for their hospital patients. Spiritual caregivers in *any* setting can appropriate this framework. Application of these tools will facilitate telling our stories, exploring perhaps more deeply and widely how the traumatic events fit into our past, our present, and our future. They will help us find connections, tell the truth, and discover ways not only to acknowledge and grieve what has been lost and what has changed but also to grasp hold of life again in richer, deeper ways.

2

COUNTING OUR WOUNDS

> Trauma is about loss of connection—to ourselves, to our bodies, to our families, to others, and to the world around us.
>
> Peter A. Levine, PhD[18]

We start with trauma (from the Greek word meaning "wound"), an injury that has the power to overwhelm. Miriam Akhtar, one of the UK's leading positive psychology practitioners, defines "traumatic experience" as the "often unexpected and uncontrollable occurrences that people feel unprepared for and powerless to prevent. These experiences provoke intense fear, horror and helplessness. Trauma poses a significant threat to our well-being."[19]

Trauma affects *all* of us. It is a fact of life. While this is a book written for caregivers to assist others through these hard times, I include all of us in this section because *no matter who we are*, the wounding of trauma and the emotions of fear and anger will impact us in our lifetime. Perhaps understanding some of these things in personal terms will bring more compassion to those for whom we minister.

Trauma works on us at multiple levels. We can start with what happens to the brain. Dr. Bessel van der Kolk, in *The Body Keeps the Score*, explains how our brains function:

> The most important job of the brain is to ensure our survival. Everything else is secondary, In order to do that, brains need to: (1) generate internal signals that register what our bodies need, such as food, rest, protection, sex, and shelter; (2) create a map of the world to point us where to go to satisfy those needs; (3) generate the necessary energy and actions to get us there; (4) warn us of dangers and opportunities along the way; and (5) adjust our actions based on the requirements of the moment...all of these imperatives require coordination and collaboration.[20]

Trauma profoundly affects all parts of our brain. The amygdala is responsible for emotions and our natural alarm system. When danger comes, it triggers a fear response for our protection. Trauma can cause it to be overactive and lowers the ability to think rationally. The neo cortex helps us reason and make decisions. The hippocampus is the area of our brain that stores and retrieves memory and shrinks in people who undergo life catastrophes. The vagus nerve carries signals from our organs to our brain. Research tells us that when the stress hormone cortisol surges into our brains it burns a path of destruction. People with severe PTSD have sustained excessively high levels of cortisol that relentlessly drive the nerve cells of the hippocampus to what might be termed "death from exhaustion." It also disrupts memory. Those experiencing trauma often do not remember the accident or illness. Because we can't remember, we can't make sense of it, and we can't put words to it. Arthur Frank, author of *The Wounded Storyteller*, writes that the narrative coherence of events and actions is "a constant task, sometimes a *struggle*, and when it succeeds it is an achievement."[21]

Trauma affects the body, too. Peter Levine asserts, "We become scared stiff, or, alternately, we collapse, overwhelmed and defeated with helpless dread. Either way, trauma defeats life."[22] Trauma shuts down growth and repair at all levels. How can you grow when you are fighting merely to breathe or move?

Fear is part of the package of trauma. Fear always comes when there is threat of loss or harm to body, mind, and spirit. It is a gift given for our survival. An emotional alarm system, it has an inherent intelligence. Something requires immediate and close attention and moves us to action to protect life. It instigates responses in us to flee, freeze, or hide and then release. This works when you are in an unsafe situation. But when illness or accident strikes, and the body is already immobilized, hanging on to fear further inhibits the body's repair work. There's no fleeing the trauma, there's no way, at least initially, to even combat what's happened. Unprocessed fear leads to anxiety and phobia.

Trauma also ignites anger, a strong emotion given to us to right wrongs, and recognize injustice. It is an appropriate response to loss. Life is unfair! What did I do to deserve this? How could God allow this? Anger that has no place to go and can't right a wrong often turns inward, causing depression.

He's on my list of new patients to see and assess. I note that he's a victim of gun violence...a devastating disease in our city....He's eighteen, and since the bullets razed his spine, his legs are paralyzed. He'll not walk again. As I approach the door, I see a sign. "Please keep this door shut AT ALL TIMES!" I knock and hear him say "Enter." There are no lights on, the TV is off, the room is dark, the blinds shut tight even though it is midday. He eyes me warily. I explain who I am and why I have come. He looks straight ahead, and barely nods at me. I can sense the tension in the room in his short breaths and straight posture, sitting up stiffly in his bed. He's very afraid, even here on the 22nd floor... afraid that someone might still come for him. Is he angry, too? Is he grieving the reality and consequences of his injury? Are there any resources from Spiritual Care that might comfort him? Does he have family support? They must be traumatized, too? I will get no answers to my questions. He's not going to talk to me, so immobilized by both physical and emotional trauma that he cannot access interventions that might assist some recovery. The visit is short. I don't want to stress him further by being in his space. I give him a list of what is offered from spiritual care, and then say "Goodbye." I leave with sadness but also hope. Perhaps through his hours of physical rehabilitation, working out with others who have similar injuries, he'll have a growing awareness that he is loved and safe, and can begin to process his situation. But not with me today.

Eventually, my patient will be returning to his community, which is also gripped and paralyzed by fear. Disease, gun violence, racism, exclusion, bullying, and prejudice are all contributing factors that ignite the dark emotions of fear, anger, and shame inherent in trauma.

Trauma disrupts the ability to form and maintain our self. It shatters illusions. All we might have dreamt about, hoped about, assumed, and pursued has been blown apart. All the *contracts* we thought we had with the world and God, about safety, about the way things work, what we can control, get washed away in the flood of damage from the trauma. As Jim Rendon puts it: "When bad things happen to someone good, it tears down that assumptive self. And much of the psychological anguish that people confront has to do with the loss of this worldview and the identity that they carried with them their entire lives."[23]

Trauma means change and loss. It makes us realize once again our humanity and our helplessness in the face of what life offers up to us. Change is a constant, nonnegotiable part of the rhythm of our lives. Nature mirrors this hard truth for us in the changing seasons: the new birth of spring, flourishing of summer, the maturity and waning of fall, the death of winter. With change comes loss. We always leave something behind. Annie Dillard asserts this truth when she writes of loss as being the price you incur by being alive, as "the extraordinary rent you have to pay as long as you stay."[24] There is potential for growth and healing, but we don't see that when we're in it.

There are many kinds of losses. **Material loss** is about losing something important to us or surroundings that made us feel secure. **Relationship loss** comes from death, divorce, leaving a group or community, being fired from a job, getting married, moving away to college, or otherwise making a big change with the people or communities in your life.

> It is the ending of opportunities to relate oneself to, talk with, share experiences with, make love to, touch, settle issues with, fight with, and otherwise be in the emotional and/or physical presence of a particular other human being. It is an unavoidable component of human life. Sooner or later we all experience such losses.[25]

There's **loss of identity**, an image that you hold of yourself, the death of a dream, or a future you had planned. Life is going to be different, and you wonder, "Who am I now?" **Functional loss** comes with disease, accident, or aging. Like many losses, this kind of loss is usually irreplaceable. Patients come into our hospital grappling with its impact, and other losses that come along side. **Intrapsychic loss** happens when a certain image of ourselves disappears, like finding out motherhood is impossible or that we can never be the actor we dreamed of being.

"Almost any trauma will bring a mixture of the types of losses mentioned above. One type may predominate, but more than one type may be felt." There are other variables as well. An avoidable loss may be harder to deal with than an unavoidable one. That is a struggle for some patients when their choices resulted in their illness or accident. If a loss is temporary, it may be easier to work through than if a loss is permanent. An anticipated loss gives us time to prepare, vs. a sudden loss. I knew for two years that my mother would die of ovarian cancer. Plenty of notice, and time to care for her, to tell her about how she had gifted my life. And still, at the funeral, I was overwhelmed with identity loss, because I was no longer able to be her daughter. Loss can be very complicated, and we do well to try to ponder all the ways it is affecting us so that we move through it and not get stuck.

Any form of loss is, at root, experienced as a loss of part of the self. A portion of the very fabric of our existence is ripped. As we work with people who are experiencing loss, it will be important to explore the types and repercussions with them. I was explaining the types of loss to a young woman who had suffered a miscarriage, thinking that she would find one or two that defined her experience. Instead, she was able to identify with many and explained to me how each had affected her. "Now I understand why this has been so hard for me!"

Trauma challenges our spirituality, both the encounter or intimate relationship with something outside ourselves and our overarching philosophy of life. The way we make choices about flourishing, ethics, and morals; how we form faith and have beliefs and practices about our meaning-making. Core beliefs and basic assumptions about God and life are violated. Faith is shattered. Identities disappear. The difficult challenges of trauma make us question everything. Balance seems unattainable.

And yet...

Robert Grant, in *The Way of the Wound*, explores how trauma impacts spirituality. He writes: "Trauma teaches! True, it teaches us about terror, helplessness. At the same time, trauma teaches us about courage, patience, compassion, and faith. Trauma calls us to wake up and pass over any seduction that shields us from realizing how short and valuable our time is on earth. Trauma teaches that life is not a pastime but a journey to wisdom. Trauma initiates conversions. It cracks open the ego and forges a link with the deepest dimensions of human consciousness."[26]

Professor Wade Mullins tweets, "Life can be shattered in a single moment…but the piecing back together requires befriending every jagged edge and sharp corner. And the scars seen in the end will tell not of the shattering, but of the resilience and value of life."[27] Lessons and insights that come in no other way will come through the experience of trauma. The person who expresses that she is all alone, sitting in the dark deserted by God, and with no way out cannot imagine that the devastation wreaked upon her will also be her ladder of escape. Never to the place she was *before* the trauma. That is gone. But launched into new ways of connection and transcendence that she could not previously have imagined or understood.

The good news is that trauma does not have to hold us hostage. The human spirit, like our bodies, was made to mend. Our spirits hold the truths we need for salvage, if only we can find ways to access them. We, as caregivers, enter this chaos. We are charged with the task of providing spiritual tools for recovery, for providing a safe, nonjudgmental, listening, loving space for people to find voice, grieve, and begin to equip for a new way forward.

3

FINDING MEANING

> Maybe nothing is more important than that we keep track, you and I, of these stories of who we are and where we have come from and the people we have met along the way because it is precisely through these stories in all their particularity, as I have long believed and often said, that God makes himself known to each of us most powerfully and personally. If this is true, it means that to lose track of our stories is to be profoundly impoverished not only humanly but spiritually.
>
> Frederick Buechner[28]

Story is the first tool. As Arthur Frank notes in *The Wounded Storyteller*:

> Stories do not simply describe the self; they are the self's medium of being....Stories have to repair the damage [from trauma] and are a way of redrawing maps and finding new destinations.[29]

It takes time to piece together—in a bearable way—the description and timeline of what happened. Even connecting to the person's past story or inserting it into the present can be challenging. I think of the patient who said, "Ok, I have Parkinson's Disease. But I'm not ready to accept what that might mean for my life." Acknowledging and accepting *all the truth* about damage received will be a slow process. But formulating our stories is so much more!

Humans have engaged in story making and telling as long as we have existed. Our stories are our most sacred possessions. The describing of experience is our most basic tool for discovery of life. Stories provide learning, problem-solving, emotional awareness, connectedness, and more. We are forced to engage within ourselves, to peel back the layers of the experience, and to find truth and meaning that informs our present and future and adds to our past. We discover the "givens" of our lives. Every post-traumatic tool is crucial to recovery. There's a reason that *story* comes first. It is the ground from which all else will spring. J. Harold Ellens, reminiscing about a traumatic childhood experience that took him from utter desolation to clear calling and purpose, wrote:

> Humans are innately driven to find life meaningful or to create meaning in it. We long for life to form a coherent picture. This need is irrepressible and universal. We intuitively and unconsciously weave all the individual stories of our lives into a meaningful master story, editing out minor or peripheral narratives and elaborating those that are central. We interpret its meaning as we go along.[30]

"Stories, no matter how simple, can be vehicles of truth; can be, in fact, icons," says Madeleine L'Engle. "Stories are able to help us to become more whole, to become Named. And Naming is one of the impulses behind all art; to give a name to the cosmos we see despite all the chaos."[31]

Whether we notice it or not, our stories shape our lives. We interpret even the most mundane events in our lives through narratives—some of which we inherit from our culture, and others that are unique to our own perceptions. Some of the most important and deeply affecting inner tales are the ones we tell about ourselves. L'Engle continues, "Without a story you haven't got a nation, or a culture, or a civilization. Without a story of your own to live you haven't got a life of your own."[32]

Recent neuroscience research affirms the importance of storytelling. Bessel Van der Kolk observes that "as soon as a story starts being told, particularly if it is told repeatedly, it changes—the act of telling itself changes the tale. The mind cannot help but make meaning out of what it knows, and the meaning we make of our lives changes how and what we remember."[33]

What can get lost in healthcare is the patient's story. Healthcare often tells its own story of the patient, a medical narrative concerned with analysis of symptoms, diagnosis, treatment. *The patient chart* can become the official story. But Arthur Frank describes a *postmodern* experience of illness where patients recognize that more is involved than the medical story can tell. The patient reclaims the telling of her own story in her own voice. A personal responsibility for oneself and others comes with this new perspective. They become witnesses to *their own experience, perspective, and truth.*

Frank proposes that there are *three underlying narratives of illness,* all of which may combine and take precedence at different times in a patient's story. All three narrative types can be used alternately and repeatedly throughout an illness.

The first is the **Restitution Narrative**. This one dominates the stories of most people who are recently ill or who suffer with chronic illness. "The plot of the restitution has the basic storyline: 'Yesterday I was healthy, today I'm sick, but tomorrow I'll be healthy again.'"[34] This story is about health. We expect we will get better. Medicine will assist the process with whatever practices the patient deems beneficial. The restitution narrative reflects our natural desire to be well and stay well and is also a culturally approved storyline.

Most aspects of our culture model this story for us. Behind TV commercials for hospitals and medicines "lies the modernist expectation that for every suffering there is a remedy."[35] The patient telling this story is reaching for predictability, a return to productivity, a future uninterrupted by illness. The body's unpredictable future with mortality, struggle, and suffering will be unacknowledged. Remedy comes by depending on agents outside of the body. It is the *first* story the patient may tell himself. It is a story that models behaviors that the patient can adopt and adapt.

But sometimes restoration or return to what was is not the next chapter. Frank asks, "What happens when those who have always spoken their own experience in the language of survival find that language has nothing left to say about themselves, once the viability of restitution has run out? What body-self is left, when the end of survival is imminent?"[36]

"Chaos is the opposite of restitution: its plot imagines life never getting better."[37] The **Chaos Narrative** is not concerned with hope or expectation for recovery. The patient is at the bottom of the pit, in the dark. There is no way out. Everything has gone wrong. Those telling and hearing these stories will experience the anxiety and the pain of life shattered and devastated. Initially, words may be insufficient. "What cannot be evaded in stories told by Holocaust witnesses," Frank observes, "is the hole in the narrative that cannot be filled in....The story traces the edges of a wound that can only be told around. Words suggest its rawness, but that wound is so much of the body, its insults, agonies, and losses, that words necessarily fail."[38] No one is in control in this storyline—not medicine, not family, certainly not the person at the middle of the trauma. The patient is going to need a lot of support in this dark place. It's going to take a long time to climb out. Frank writes that "the greatest chaos stories are the first despairing verses of many of the Psalms; the Psalms' message seems to be that the redemption of faith can begin only in chaos....For the poor in spirit to recognize their blessedness, some reflective space is required."[39] And that is where we as chaplains and caregivers can provide unmeasurable support.

The **Quest Narrative** acknowledges the suffering, finds meaning, and uses the lessons learned in the experience. This narrator finds her own voice, tells her own story. While restitution and chaos remain in the background and become part of the story, the patient can begin to see her story as a journey. She can place this experience within her larger story and find a way to move forward. New light begins to come. Out of her suffering, a bigger life context emerges. Suffering is no longer imprisonment in the dark, but a way to new understanding and compassion that extends to others. Transformation is possible. Not to life as it was, but new life with potential for forward movement, wisdom, and previously unimagined flourishing.

"Tell me about you," I ask.

And the elderly patient (I'll call her Ivy) begins her story. It is a long life with mention of brothers and sisters, children, her long struggle with arthritis, her church family and friends, her belief in God. She tells me her daughter wants her to come to Atlanta to live with her, but she resists because her community is here. "I'd be all alone down there," she observes.

But I know this is not the reason she wants to talk to me. I sit there waiting.

She tells me about the aunt she spent years taking care of. How her family felt she was wasting her own life dedicated to the aunt. "She didn't have anyone else. She didn't have any children to take care of her. I felt it was my responsibility," she says. "And she died not long ago."

I wonder to myself whether it is adjustment of returning to her own life...no longer being needed? Or is it grief that the aunt has passed? I explore this, but that's not it.

And then her face contorts, and her eyes get teary. "At the funeral I became almost paralyzed," she relates. "They had to get a wheelchair to take me home. Right at the funeral! Suddenly, I couldn't even close my hand. Why did that happen to me?"

"You feel punished for your good work, don't you?" She nods, looking down. "All those years of serving your aunt, sacrificing for her, obeying God, and this is your payment!" She nods again. I don't know why this has happened, but I can see it's a big problem for her. We talk about the "why?" question. It is part of our humanity to ask *why* things happen when life turns a corner we don't expect. We talk about suffering. She holds up one hand, opens it, and closes it. "But look at me," she says. I've been making good progress here. "They've extended my stay. God is good to me, but I still don't understand why that happened to me at the funeral." She looks away, out the window.

"You want to find the meaning of your attack at that particular time, don't you?" "Yes," she nods, "I want to make meaning." She requests that I read the "times" from Ecclesiastes to her. I slowly read them, and she repeats each line after me. She wants to think about each one...a time to grieve and a time to dance...a time to scatter stones and a time to gather stones...a time to be quiet and a time to speak. When I finish, I look at her. She's sitting with her eyes closed. "You could tell me a story about every one of those times, couldn't you?" She nods. I think she's chosen Ecclesiastes, hoping to find wisdom and answer for her question.

This has been a good visit so far. But I know we haven't solved her dilemma. "What did you pray for while you were taking care of your aunt?" I ask.

She says, "Well, I prayed that God would keep me moving in spite of my pain, so I could take care of her. If I got sick no one else would have...." She stops and looks at me. I see some kind of flash go across her face. She leans back, relieved, in her wheelchair.

"What are you thinking, Ivy?"

Slowly she says, "God answered my prayer! God kept me well enough to take care of her, and then she died." "Are you saying God kept you from becoming incapacitated with your arthritis so you could care for her...and now...now you've time for surgery and treatment to help you recover? You didn't have that time before." She looks at me intently. "I think we've got something," she says slowly, a smile spreading across her face.

Ivy was searching for meaning in her life; she was involved in quest narrative, looking for answers to her "why" questions. As she narrated her story to me, she became able to view it from a different perspective. When that new idea of "why" she had suffered hit her, she visibly relaxed, and gave a big sigh of relief. Now she can emotionally and spiritually engage in her physical recovery. She is no longer weighed down by grief and confusion. Her positive outlook will contribute to her enthusiasm and progress in rehabilitation.

How do we facilitate a person's quest narrative? To begin to heal, we must discover ways of expressing how our shattered bodies, minds, and spirits have been impacted. That can be really difficult at first, almost like reliving the past again. But this truth telling is the place to start. Martin Buber says, "We can be redeemed only to the extent to which we see ourselves."[40] Language must be found that begins to name the wounding and its accompanying losses. Think carefully about words chosen in the narration. Encourage hopeful language: "I can." "I will." "It's possible...." Stories will include acknowledging the loss that the trauma brought. Tedeschi and Calhoun suggest that deliberate rumination is helpful in this process.

> It is not wallowing or obsessing. When someone is deliberately ruminating on a problem, he is actively involved in thinking about how the event has impacted him, what it means for him, and how he can live his life going forward given the challenges that the event has posed...deliberate rumination is the way that people begin to rebuild themselves.[41]

Emotions and actions issue directly from beliefs about what happened or the experience of trauma. Are those beliefs accurate? True? Whatever narrative the person tells, that is the place to start. The narrative may not really be true. But it is truth to them in the moment of telling. Eventually, if the person is given space for the exploration of feelings, timelines, and experience, real truth will come and be powerful. Can a plan for the future be laid out at this point? Probably not. Can they find all the answers to their questions? No, but insight and meaning-making will come. The quest narrative can be a long process...it is a journey! It opens up the doorway to new ways of thinking and doing. Meanwhile, there's work to be done right here, right now.

With loss comes grief. It comes like a flood, bringing a multitude of emotions, not just one, but many, which makes it overwhelming and difficult to sort through. "Emotions live in the body," Miriam Greenspan notes pointedly. "They explode us into ecstasy or devour us with pain. They make us fidget and squirm, surge with adrenaline, or go numb and lifeless. They affect the rate at which our hearts beat and the level and balance of various hormones, influencing the way that we breathe, think, work, digest our food, make love."[42] Supporting the grief process will be one of the major interventions offered by caregivers.

How do we begin to cope with the reaction and overwhelming conflict of feelings that come with loss? John Donne, the English poet and priest who lived and died during the Black Plague, wrote: "He who lacks time to mourn, lacks time to mend." If every change brings loss, then everyone has some level of grieving to do. There is a saying that "all therapy is grief work." Grief implicates our whole existence. In some ways, it never resolves. Some psychologists say closure is a myth, that losses will always retain the power to evoke previous losses. It disrupts our narrative... it will become part of our story...but only after a lot of struggle. "Human illness, even when lived as a quest, always returns to mourning. The boon is gaining the ability to mourn not for oneself only, but for others."[43] Our own suffering becomes a catalyst for loving and sharing with others. We realize that we all suffer, and none of us can bear it alone. It is one of the greatest gifts that comes out of this painful place...the new awareness of others and a greater ability to love.

There is no single process by which we adjust to loss, nor is there a set time frame in which we must mourn. Grief is the process of letting go. Grief is the struggle to retrieve ourselves and our meaning-making capacity.

We grieve alone. We grieve with family and friends over mutual losses. Grief is called *collective* when it is felt by a community, society, village, or nation from an event such as war, natural disaster, terrorist attack, death of a public figure, or any other event leading to mass casualties or national tragedy. Our world is presently grieving wounds and losses from the pandemic, the wars in Ukraine, Israel, and Gaza, our polarized political environment and more.

Think about the cumulative grief of a patient who is in the hospital because of an auto accident in which his wife died, and now because of his injuries, may never go home again but to a care facility—and because of his injuries, may lose his job. Or think about the displaced refugee, losing home, community, and perhaps a husband or child to war. Or think about the mother, imprisoned in poverty, her child murdered or paralyzed by gunshot, with seemingly no way up or out. Trauma brings experiences of transition and change that may pile on top of one another, building stress and causing grief and loss that must be acknowledged. As caregivers, we come with awareness of *our own pain and loss*, and the compassion that arises out of that understanding. We grieve *with* those we care for. By understanding the different kinds of grief and loss, in touch with our own, we more deeply assist the exploration of wounding and its repercussions on the individuals we minister to.

Invite lament as part of the storytelling. It becomes an important part of the narrative. We speak of our struggles and suffering. The world is not as it ought to be! It's not fair! We challenge the status quo and cry out for justice. We protest. We tell what we have experienced. And most importantly, we direct our sorrows outward and upward to God.

The Psalms are a good resource for this. They have been described as the "anatomy of the soul." The lament psalms range from deep alienation to profound trust, confidence, and gratitude. Many times, reading the words of a psalm appropriate to a patient's experience has brought comfort and solace. I've used them for celebration and recovery as well.[44]

On this day I receive a page: "Please see patient in room _____ asap." It is signed by the physician. There is no attached information. I respond immediately, and as I come to the door, the doctor is leaving the room. "He needs to see you, I think," she says. "We've tried the psychologist and nothing else has worked. Please go on in." The patient (I'll call him Ed) is in bed. I do not know the details of his illness. I didn't take time to pull up his chart. His daughter is beside his bed, and as I introduce myself, she immediately stands up and says, "I'll step out, Dad. See you later." I assure her she's welcome to stay. But I sense frustration from her, too, like the doctor. She wants a break and is anxious for me to "take over" for a while. And he seems ready to talk to me. He waves goodbye to her and motions me closer to the bed.

His bed is tilted up slightly; the sheets are pulled up across his chest, under his arms. There is nothing that gives me a clue to his physical situation. However, his face is wet with tears. Where should I begin?

I lean over the guardrail as a chair is too low and too far away to talk to him. "What's wrong?" I ask.

"I just can't stop crying," he whimpers. "Ever since my accident in April [it's now June] I've been crying and I can't stop!" His face twists up and gets red, as a fresh round of tears fall down his cheeks. He begins the story of his fall, his injured back and leg, his surgery, his inability to recover enough to participate in therapy. He can't bring himself to get out of bed.

"This has turned your life upside down," I observe. He nods, sniffling. It occurs to me that he might fully need to put voice to what appears to be a multitude of plaints about his present situation. I know there is power in naming emotions and paying attention to his truth in this moment. There is also healing in being listened to. Ed needs to do some truth telling.

So I encourage him to expand on how this has affected him and his family. He tells me of the burden on his family. He's bothered that they have to sit with him in the hospital. He's disrupted their lives. His wife is ill, and he can't take care of her. He's become the problem. He's let everyone down. He can't get better. He's the leader of his family, the strong one, and now he's the one that needs help.

I ask lots of questions to help open up his litany of grief. "What does it feel like to helplessly lie here? In what ways has this affected your wife and your family? How does your family feel about your illness? What do you feel is lost and may not be recovered? How has this changed your life? Do you have any hope for recovery?" I hear elements of anger, sadness, outrage, hopelessness, guilt, frustration, and shame in his responses.

We continue for some time, and at some point in the conversation, he wonderingly observes, "I'm not crying!" I nod, but I don't stop pushing him to verbalize everything weighing on his heart.

When it seems we have exhausted this conversation, we sit in silence a while. He's lying there, spent, I think, with his long accounting. I ask his permission to read a psalm. He nods his assent. I realize that I haven't heard him mention God. He hasn't once said, "Why did God allow this?" or "God has deserted me!" as some patients do. But does that matter? We'll use the Psalms as a way to negotiate through dark places he's in. Maybe it will help Ed find his way.

I read from Psalm 69 that begins, "Save me, O God, for the waters have come up to my neck. I sink in deep mire, where there is no foothold; I have come into deep waters, and the flood sweeps over me. I am weary with my crying...." Does he identify with this? I look up at him from my Bible. He's listening closely and nods as he seems to recognize shadows of his own situation. I skip down to verse 13, "But as for me, my prayer is to you, O Lord. At an acceptable time, O God, in the abundance of your steadfast love, answer me. With your faithful help rescue me from sinking in the mire." I end with verses 16–18, "Answer me, O Lord, for your steadfast love is good....Draw near to me, redeem me, set me free."

He's resting quietly now. There are no tears. "Would it be alright if I offer a prayer for you?" I ask. He nods and reaches out his hand for me to hold. And so, in my prayer, we write *his* psalm. I name again the major themes of his lament. I call on the promises, the power, and the love of God. I say, "You are the God who stretches out the starry curtain of the heavens. You placed the world in its foundation. You made the mountains and the streams, and caused the plants to grow. And You have promised that you will rescue us. You will be with us in trouble. You will satisfy us with a long life and give us your salvation. Ed needs to feel your presence, Lord!" I petition God to relieve this man of his discouragement, to bring strength and healing, to set him on a new path so that he can embrace his future.

When I finish, he smiles and gives me a firm handshake. "I'm so thankful that you came. You have really helped me. I don't think I need to cry *anymore*! I think I'm ready to rest now." He's at peace, ready to rest, and cheerfully gets up for therapy the next morning.

Ed needed to tell his story, to lay all the facets of it on the table. He was holding a lot of shame and grief about his inability to provide and care for his family. He needed to lament and grieve all his losses, which were many. We took the time to name all of the wounds and concerns he was holding. We explored them in depth. And because he was able to put words to them and to his feelings, he was able to let go enough that it relieved his emotional trauma and paralysis. That release spawned a new freedom, enabling him to get up from his sickbed and participate in therapy.

Ivy's work was about finding meaning. Ed's was much more about naming what had paralyzed him and had caused the continual tears. For both, telling their story was integral to moving them toward healing.

Elisabeth Kübler-Ross named the stages of grief as denial or numbness, anger, bargaining, depression, and acceptance.[45] Current understanding and experience teaches us that grief is chaos.

THE "STAGES OF GRIEF"

REALITY

All these "stages" may be present in no particular order and at the same time. Grief is not just one emotion, there are many: sadness, anger, regret, fear, shame, relief, and more, which is why it feels like a tidal wave and causes such inability to cope.

Contemporary research explores grief instead from the perspective of narrative disruption. Grief has caused one's story to take a left turn. There is a forced reevaluation of life beliefs and assumptions. Grief will reorder the future; it may violate basic presuppositions about the laws of the universe. Robert Neimeyer names "reconstruction of a world of meaning," as more helpful to understanding grief than the passive endurance of stages.[46] This is where the story tool is so valuable. It is out of this evaluation of experience, naming of loss, exploration of grief with all its emotions, and insertion into the existing storyline that meaning-making and healing will begin to come.

Grief is experienced in mind, heart, spirit, and body. It is *normal* for it to affect all of us. It is a personal experience and our losses don't have to be validated by others. The task of grief is to accept the reality of the loss. What has been lost and what has not? Who am I now? How am I changed? Identities and relationships will change with whatever was lost. Building the new narrative helps the adjustment to the new, true reality of life. As caregivers, we can help make space for negative words and thoughts, sometimes too difficult to share with family. We make space for gratitude and forgiveness, too, interpersonal strengths that produce well-being.[47]

If we can look back at a life that was lost, and find gratefulness for the gifts given us by that life, from that life, we will be more likely to move through grief instead of getting stuck there.

Ask: "What can be recovered?" It's not about forgetting what came before but acknowledging new identities. And as energy turns toward the future, the question becomes, "How will I go on?" And even if the future is about end of life, there's still work to be done. There is life review: "What do you need to let go of?"

"What are you grateful for?" "What do you regret?" "What do you want your family to know or understand?" "What preparations do you still need to make for what's next?" "Is there anything left undone that you could still repair?" All the tools of growth after trauma aid this process. As story forms, we ask these questions: "Who is willing to hear me?" "Who can I tell my story to?" And that's how we come to the next tool: community.

4

GATHERING SUPPORT

> None of us comes into the world fully formed. We would not know how to think, or walk, or speak, or behave as human beings unless we learned it from other human beings. We need other human beings in order to be human. I am because other people are....The solitary, isolated human being is really a contradiction in terms.
>
> Desmond Tutu[48]

> When you share your story of struggle, you offer me companionship in mine, and that's the most powerful soul medicine I know.
>
> Parker Palmer[49]

Of all the many wounds of the COVID-19 pandemic, perhaps one of the greatest was the prohibition of embodiment, being together, benefitting from hugs and physical affection. People died alone, celebrations and rituals were cancelled, churches and schools closed their doors. Life became isolated and confined. Togetherness, always perceived as an opportunity for health and growth, became the dire threat to our existence. Perhaps for the first time, we realized how important we are to one another. Wendell Berry says, "Community is the knowledge that people have of each other, their concern for each other, their trust in each other, the freedom with which they come and go among themselves."[50]

Community is a big word. It stretches from a one-on-one encounter to a family, a group, a city, a culture, a country, and even our world. We were *made* for community. Right from the start, God said so. Martin Buber writes: "All real living is meeting."[51] Community or group work accomplishes what cannot be done alone. Judith Herman, one of the first clinicians to put labels to prolonged, repeated trauma, argues that healing from trauma "is more than a private, individual matter. Restorative justice comes from acknowledgment, apology, and amends, which can be delivered through community."[52] Being with others challenges perspective, gives encouragement, provides a mirror, and meets practical needs. It is a place where we can give and receive support while growing the courage to ask for help. It is the place to tell stories, name emotions, discover gifts and talents that can be used for us and one another. It helps name and frame identity. It encourages looking beyond our selves and brings compassion. We learn to be in relationship, see how alike and different we are,

trust enough to have others check on us, ask hard questions, call us to accountability. It grows resilience, validation, and rehabilitation. We should be able to laugh, brainstorm, consult, cry, and become better persons as a result of our communities.

The challenge of this tool is that it's not simply about getting together. There are long-term factors that have inhibited communities from growing in the ways they were meant to serve us. Another challenge is that over centuries, communities have wounded and disserved us as well. The pandemic highlighted and exacerbated racial inequities that continue to exist in some of our marginalized communities. Enterprise Community Partners of Chicago, whose mission is to "make home and community places of pride, power, and belonging," reports:

> The long history of racial inequities in the U.S. has left communities deprived of an environment that supports holistic healing. This deprivation has become more apparent and exacerbated by Covid-19, which has unveiled a reality that society has chosen to ignore. Repeatedly, disproportionate amounts of trauma and adverse outcomes on the Black and Indigenous people from natural disasters, pandemics, violence and economic challenges have proven to have a root cause in racism.[53]

Many initiatives in our cities have been birthed from the compassionate recognition of ongoing wounding. Our city governments, nonprofits, independent groups, and churches are hard at work attempting to hear, acknowledge and address these issues and to offer resources and support for community to work as it was meant to.[61]

Dr. Judith Herman, exploring pathways to justice and healing in her book *Truth and Repair*, writes:

> I propose that survivors of violence, who know in their bones the truths that many others would prefer not to know, can lead the way to a new understanding of justice. The first step is simply to ask survivors what would make things right—or as right as possible—for them. This sounds like such a reasonable thing to do, but in practice, it is hardly ever done. Listening, therefore, turns out to be a radical act.[54]

This attentive "seeing and listening," whether offered by an individual caregiver or a group, may be the first step in the journey toward recovery. Clinical psychologist Dr. Arielle Schwartz affirms this:

> We adapt to adversity by orienting to our strengths, attending to our pain, and taking charge of the narrative that defines our lives. I believe that we all have the capacity to overcome adversity. However, this requires that we have compassionate support and intelligent guidance. Our injuries do not occur in a vacuum, so our healing cannot occur in one either. Our hurts and losses need to be repaired interpersonally. We cannot heal alone.[55]

Listening is perhaps the most important gift community offers us. Miriam Greenspan, whose birthplace and first home was in a camp for refugees after the Holocaust, is passionate about the importance of listening: "Without a listener, the healing process is aborted. Human beings, like plants that bend toward the sunlight, bend toward others in an innate healing tropism. There are times when being truly listened to is more critical than being fed."[56] We need loving, hospitable, nonjudgmental receivers of our stories, our pain, our doubts, our truth, and our suffering.

How do we listen well in a way that fosters healing? One key fact to remember is that if you are talking, you are not listening!

Spiritual directors and counselors learn that "there are two ways to give a person the opportunity to tell their story. One way is by open-ended questions,"[57] such as, "Can you say more about that?" "Can you give me an example?" "What was that like for you?" "I'm wondering about…" "What are you making of all this?" "Have you talked to God about this?" "The second, and more difficult, way is through silence."[58] This simple act of staying quiet and waiting allows the speaker to think, make connections, notice their feelings, or go deeper into their own experience. Often there are no real words that are good enough for the pain someone is going through. Even if your words are not what you think they should be sometimes, your compassionate presence will be healing. Your responses ought to invite the person to put words to their pain and reflect on what is happening inside them—this is the start of their grief work. It is not the time for conclusions, advice, answers, or telling of your own experience.

We reflect, paraphrase, mirror as we listen to their stories. It is in these first encounters where the person begins to put words to their injury that we will assist in opening the door to recovery. This process is not about just finding words, formulating a timeline, acknowledging reality and truth in the story. What we can help a person or group do is *accommodate and assimilate* the new information, build a new worldview, make the trauma foundational to a new future.

In listening to a person's testimony, spiritual caregivers offer a nonjudgmental, welcoming presence, perspective, and space that isn't often available through the family, hospital clinical staff, or social agencies. As the survivor interacts with others, the sense of belonging and safety brings empowerment and security as he realizes he is not alone. Others' suffering and insights contribute to his own understanding and growth.

Trauma causes social distancing, disrupted participations in life, the ability to love, trust, and be intimate. Community is important for all of us, but for one whose life has been turned upside down, with many relationship connections altered or severed, community can play a huge role in recovery. The benefits play out in many ways. Social support is a powerful factor in helping people recover from post-traumatic stress symptoms and PTSD, too. A 2019–2020 research study on moral injury and suicidal behavior among U.S. combat veterans documented that the single best predictor of post-traumatic growth was the level of social support the soldiers had following his or her deployment:

> Social support is not the same as merely being in the presence of others. Your story telling must occur in a safe, non-judgmental space, where love, with its steadfastness, tenderness, commitment, and forgiveness can be present and offered, the sharing given and received in confidence with compassion. Being loved and listened to with regard and respect, we develop the ability to love and have compassion for others. It is a process of being known and seen, having our feelings and thoughts validated. For our physiology to calm down, heal, and grow we need a visceral feeling of safety.[59]

Benefit also comes from being with "those who understand what the survivor is going through, who the individual feels he can be open with."[60]

How can we offer the empowerment of community and social support in the hospital environment? There's the "one-on-one" with us chaplains; there's the engagement of family and interaction with medical staff. But at my hospital, we felt there was more we could do. We laid the post-traumatic growth tools over our practice and decided that one thing missing from the interventions of our department was group support work. One group that formed because of this discernment was the Limb Loss Group. The encounter below describes how this dynamic worked simply by bringing patients together.

On this Wednesday, the chaplain in charge begins by welcoming the five new patients who have wheeled in and made a circle. He invites them to introduce themselves. Each patient readily takes a turn, moving into their story of illness and loss resulting in the loss of a limb. Feelings, thoughts, grief, and physical difficulties are named. Heads nod in sympathy as each person recounts their medical journey to this point. All respectfully wait for the speaker to finish before the next one starts their own story.

Sometimes it is quiet for a moment as people react to what has been said. Some reach over to pat a shoulder as they recount pain and loss. One woman begins to cry quietly and continues to weep as conversation continues. "I haven't cried about this before. I didn't realize how much I needed to. It's important for me to get this out," she gestures at herself, holding her wad of Kleenex. At the end of the meeting, she reports that she feels so much clearer, and less burdened by her situation.

The chaplain asks how it feels to be so vulnerable, and there is a collective sigh. All agree that while their loss has forced them to be vulnerable, there is a strength in their willingness to ask for help, to accept kindness from others, and to accept their present situation. One patient with a good voice had declined when asked to sing at the beginning of the group, but by this point she says, "I'm ready to sing now," then launches into a lyrical spiritual: "Everything's Gonna Be All Right." The other patients clap along.

The hour is nearly up. The patients have shared, cried, and encouraged one another. "This was great! Could we do this again next week?" they ask. They wheel out, back to their respective rooms, newly bonded, and maybe even with new friendships that outlast their stays.

A week later, two of the men have bonded so much that they have exchanged contact information and plan to stay in touch. One of these men, eyes downcast and silent in the previous meeting, is now interceding for others and speaking clearly of his experience of loss. The woman whose son is dying of cancer asks for prayer from all of us. We scoot forward, wheelchairs and all, hold hands, and one of the new participants prays for her. Another woman declares, "When I went out into the therapy lab the next morning after our meeting, I saw you all around and working, and I realized, 'I have family here!'"

Everything that community offers was present in that hour. With a little direction and space provided by the chaplain, this group of people was able to grieve, bond, offer compassion to one another, affirm faith, and find solace and emotional, spiritual healing. All left in a "better place."

The dynamics of healing inherent in group work kicked in that afternoon. And, as you may notice, it was with minimal facilitation of the leader. The group did its own work.

Another important intervention for a person emerging from trauma is to assess support for reentry into their own community. Who will be there for them? How do family, friends, church, social groups, work colleagues and perhaps neighbors fit into a coherent plan for all that community must offer? The simple tool listed at the back in Resources is a good aid for this discussion. A page handout with concentric circles on it can assist a patient to look forward to how she will rejoin her communities. Invite the patient to consider and prioritize her circles of support. Some questions to ask: What are your circles of support? What order would you assign them? Is there a group that's not working for you? Is there a group you should add? Is your faith or your church a source of support? Where are you in your circles of support?

Here's how it worked for one patient:

"Bill" was a patient with amputation of both legs. I was called to his room because he had just received word that his wife wanted a divorce. With tears running down his face, he talked of his desperation. What was he going to do? Who would help him? How would he go on? We chatted for quite a while.

At the end of our visit, I gave him the "circles of support" worksheet. "Bill, take a look at this if you have time. Maybe it will help you determine what support you do have available or what you might need to add in." I left, planning to see him the next day. I didn't really expect him to do anything with the worksheet.

The next day as I entered his room, he held up the sheet. There was writing all over it. "Tell me about this!" I said in amazement.

"Well," he said, "I started working on this." He pointed enthusiastically to the circles. "I have my friends here, and I have some family here. And I have my church family. They are on this circle." He points at the worksheet, listing far more people than I might have dreamed were available to him. "I have my wife on this outer circle, because she's still paying the bills," he adds, with a wistful smile.

"So, Bill, what do you make of this?" I asked. He leaned back triumphantly in his chair: "I didn't realize how loved I was! I'm going to be all right. I can do this!"

Bill will be able to move forward from his loss because he has realized he has good support around him. He will utilize these relationships as he processes his losses and pursues his physical and emotional recovery.

Rituals are another way to offer community. They help us express joy and sorrow, celebration and loss, letting go and taking in. All people in all cultures are profoundly ritualistic. They mark our days, our cycles of time, our endings and beginnings, and usher us forward out of liminal waiting periods. They may be as simple as a pizza night or as formal as the swearing in of a new president; as religious as a Mass or as personal as brushing your teeth before bed. Graduations, funerals, dedicating a building, baptizing a child—we use rituals to mark whatever is significant to us.

We affirm our identity and our experience through ritual. We tell the truth of the moment. We can be comforted, be given permission to express feelings, bring a sense of closure, or keep an important part of the past alive. A trauma survivor may not yet have found a way to put together the fragments of memories and identity and worldview. Yet via ritual, they are immersed in and surrounded by a community that is present to them and available when they come to a point where they can begin to tell their story.

To mark these specific experiences for people, you can prepare by asking the following questions:[61]

1. What are we ritualizing?
2. What is the primary function of the ritual? (Truth telling, celebrating, consoling...)
3. Who will be there?
4. What symbolic actions would express this experience most meaningfully? (Dance, song, writing notes, lighting a candle, making a sign, etc.)
6. What do we want to say? Who should say it?
7. In what order should we do all these things? What is the natural emotional flow? What is the natural physical flow? What leads us toward the end in mind?

Here is a basic outline for a ritual:[62]

1. **Gathering:** Why have you come together?
2. **Telling (storytelling):** What are the facts of your pain or loss? How does it feel? We will not always feel this way, but this is how we feel now.
3. **Taking Action:** Symbolize what's happened by

lighting a candle, joining hands, tearing up a letter, choosing a rock, writing a word...there are numerous ways to act creatively in the action taking. Proclaim hope, not mere optimism. Acknowledge mutuality of experience, or faith, or beliefs.

4. **Sending:** Ask for blessing, ask for change or healing, voice hope for the future.

A sense of presence and care can be delivered to patients in many ways. At our hospital, because of the generosity and work of the Kenilworth Union Church Knitting Club, we can introduce another key gift of community to patients. They supply us with colorful lap robes accompanied by a hand-signed greeting card and prayer for the patient's recovery. The prayer says, in part, "May this lap robe be a sign for you of God's healing presence... may it warm you when you are weary and surround you with holy peace." The reception of these robes is hugely positive. One patient told me, "I am keeping this for my whole life." Another reported that not only does he sleep with his lap robe, he also insists that it stays around his shoulders during his therapies. Patients keep the cards, and some write thank-you notes back to the group. This intervention inspires gratefulness, a sense of being loved and "seen," and has opened the door to conversation with patients who might otherwise not have welcomed or trusted conversation with a chaplain. Here's how it impacted one patient:

I visit a woman coping with cancer, whose hospital bed somehow collapsed and hurt her spine. Now she is here in our rehab hospital with no feeling in her legs, hoping for some recovery. I go in to introduce myself, welcome her, and find out how spiritual care might support her. "Do you come from any faith or cultural background?" "Baptist," she replies curtly. "Would you be interested in attending our Sunday morning service?" "No." "Would you like a Bible?" "I don't think so." I can see that she is discouraged and scared. She is looking out the window as she answers. My challenge is to get to a place where she might trust me and be willing to do some work together. "Would you mind if I come and visit you occasionally?" "No, I don't need that, but thank you for coming," she says politely but dismissively. So, I have one more tool in my box. "What is your favorite color?" I ask. She turns to me, willing to engage for the first time. "Well, it used to be dark blue, but now I've kind of turned to black because it goes with everything," she explains.

Ah! This is who the black lap robe has been waiting on! There's been a beautiful black lap robe in the supply room, and it just hasn't been the right one for anyone so far. I tell her I'll be right back. And I can tell she's intrigued about what I am bringing her. I return and spread the black, sparkly ruffled robe over her lap. I tell her, "This is from the Kenilworth Union Church Knitting Club. These ladies knit these, bless them, and bring them to us for patients here at the hospital." I show her the card with the women's signatures and read their message that this comes to her with a big hug and prayer for her recovery. She silently takes it, strokes it, holds it up to her heart....And then looks heavenward and shouts: "Oh, thank you, Jesus! This is just what I needed! Thank you! Thank you! Oh, my goodness, I needed this and didn't even know I needed it! Thank you!" she declares passionately and tears stream down her face.

Her reaction surprised me. I expected that she might like it, but the gift did more. It opened the door to additional visits, reconnection with her faith, and receptivity for many other therapies. The knitting group loves to hear the stories of reception of their lap robes, and they report to me that their group has grown because of the giving and receiving that occurs in these exchanges. It's just another way community heals us.

Its work brings the courage to hope. Parker Palmer writes: "Imparting hope to others has nothing to do with exhorting or cheering them on. It has everything to do with relationships that honor the soul, encourage the heart, inspire the mind, quicken the step, and heal the wounds we suffer along the way."[63] The gift of presence is primary. As one grieving parent wrote:

> If you think your task as comforter is to tell me that really, all things considered, it's not so bad, you do not sit with me in my grief but place yourself off in the distance away from me. Over there, you are of no help. What I need to hear from you is that you recognize how painful it is. I need to hear...that you are with me in my desperation. To comfort me, you have to come close. Come sit beside me.[64]

5

ENGAGING POWER

> The new dawn blooms as we free it. For there is always light, if only we're brave enough to see it. If only we're brave enough to be it.
>
> Amanda Gorman[65]

> Hope, I have come to believe, is as vital to our lives as the very oxygen that we breathe.
>
> Jerome Groopman[66]

Hope simply and powerfully offers and energizes a pathway to healing. Like other "positive emotions"—love, joy, awe, and gratefulness—hope infuses us with expectation for recovery and flourishing. And like the other tools mentioned so far, hope has a particular power to move us up and forward out of the mire of trauma. It is a generative emotion that manages fear and provides "a ballast that keeps us steady."[67]

Unfortunately, trauma teaches helplessness. Helplessness can kill hope. When that slide into the dark happens, we can forget that we are loved, that we have support, and that we can still choose life.

"How do you find hope?" asks the chaplain. "What do you hope for from here?"

The Limb Loss Group starts a new round of comments, as they name faith, family support, getting prosthetics so they can walk again, gratefulness for what remains of their bodies. One woman, without a particularly defined faith, says, "I hope to see the sun rise another day, to see beautiful flowers, to go home again." She continues, "I wish there were a way we could help each other." And another says, "Having this group and talking together has been a great help!" Others nod "yes." They agree together that they have chosen life at the cost of the limb loss.

Hope lights a way to the future and brings the *will* to change. We lost many valuable supports during the Pandemic and one of those was hope. That prompted people to start looking and writing about it during COVID's worst days. In a *Wall Street Journal* article in 2020, entitled "Finding Hope When Everything Else Feels Hopeless," Elizabeth Bernstein wrote,

> Hope is crucial to our physical and mental health. It guards against anxiety and a sense of futility. And it protects us from stress: Research shows that '"people with higher levels of hope"' have better coping skills and bounce back from setbacks faster. They're better at problem-solving and have lower levels of burnout. They have stronger relationships, because they communicate better and are more trusting.[68]

Community is key. We need one another's company to climb out of the pit of despair. It is often others who hold hope when the individual cannot. The article went on to quote Anthony Scioli who called hope the "Personal Protective Emotion" (PPE) and notes resources that emanate from community:

> First comes attachment, a sense of continued trust and connection. Next is mastery, or empowerment, a

> feeling of being strong and capable. Survival is third and has two features—a belief that you aren't trapped in a bad situation, and an ability to hold on to positive thoughts and feelings. Fourth is spirituality, a belief in something larger than yourself. Research says that patients who are hopeful, largely because of their religious faith and their trust in the physician, have a more rapid return to health and a higher rate of survival.[69]

A patient in the Limb Loss Group says, "You've all lost limbs, and you are surviving. Maybe I can, too." Shared experience brings comfort. To see others existing and coping with the same ailments also opens up possibility. The love and compassion of others provides a platform for imagining that there is something ahead that might take place, whether it is hope for healing, hope for alleviation of pain, or even hope for a good death. It is about developing the ability to look forward instead of backward.

Hope engenders choice. Choosing to hope provides a new sense of control, lost in the traumatic events of the past. Hope motivates, encouraging us to choose life, to seek food, therapy, and other tools for recovery. Embedded in the human spirit is the desire to anticipate and grasp a *realistic* future. Not wishful thinking, or false hope. "False hope does not recognize the risks and dangers that true hope does.... True hope takes into account the real threats that exist and seeks to navigate the best path around them."[70] It is rooted in reality, even if that reality seems very daunting. It permits us to focus on specific issues and outcomes. It powers goalsetting, building the path forward.

Reward circuits, rich in dopamine, get ignited when we set goals. Willpower and way power kick in. Anticipation comes. Dreams form. Conflict resolution, the weighing of opposing choices, ways to proceed, utilizing past experience, all open new patterns for health instead of negative rumination. The value of hope extends beyond simply helping us to achieve our goals. Hope works alongside story, but not only as a cognitive emotion or skill but to rebuild identity.

Physician Jerome Groopman describes how hope affects our brains and our bodies: "When we feel pain from our physical debility, that pain amplifies our sense of hopelessness; the less hopeful we feel, the fewer endorphins and enkephalins and the more CCK we release. The more pain we experience due to these neurochemicals, the less able we are to feel hope."[71]

Fortunately for us, our bodies were made to mend. Some things are lost, but the body works constantly to repair. Muscles can strengthen, minds can develop new channels, infections can be cleared. The first spark of hope can help break the pain cycle. "Hope helps us overcome hurdles that we otherwise could not scale, and it moves us forward to a place where healing can occur."[72] Groopman likens it to a "natural form of morphine" and observes the steps:

> Hope sets off a chain reaction. Hope tempers pain, and as we sense less pain, that feeling of hope expands, which further reduces pain. As pain subsides, a significant obstacle to enduring a harsh but necessary therapy is removed....The stirrings of recovery in our tissues help generate the feeling of hope....With each increment in improvement, the body sends more signals that inform the brain of a return to health....Even the smallest reduction in the symptom of fatigue also has a major impact on the patient's sense of hope.[73]

Hopefulness feeds recovery. From secular and religious perspectives, hope is *the* emotion that enables the way forward out of adversity. Called a virtue by ancient Greeks, for people of faith, it is

> an essential component of appreciating the transcendent...an enduring attitude related to the belief in God's

> goodness and power to bring good out of desperate circumstances, even if these circumstances fail to demonstrably change in the here and now. This notion relies not so much on one's strength, but on the help of the grace offered by God.[74]

Spiritually, worship, prayer, and meditation are a means of increasing one's mental energy or willpower. These practices recharge mind and body, provide mental rest and renewal and the ways and means to realize new pathways. Hope becomes a form of sustenance for us and those around us.

Hope is contagious. We can encourage one another's measure of hope. That was an obvious dynamic in our small groups, as patients shared together. It inspires a stronger spirituality and often provides a way to reunion and reactivation of religious beliefs and faith shattered in the trauma.

Memory is another element in summoning and sustaining hope. Hope integrates information and feelings derived from present circumstances, and it also draws on experiences of the past, seeking models and directions from other individuals who endured and transcended harrowing situations and overcame seemingly long odds.

Swiss theologian Emil Brunner writes: "What oxygen is for the lungs, such is hope for the meaning of human life."[75] So with all this power, what deters hope? One of the greatest obstacles is fear. This gift given to our lives for protection, to freeze, flee, or hide when danger presents itself is not an emotion to be held.

The patient is sitting up in her bed, tears coming down her cheeks. "What's wrong?" I inquire.

"I can't get up for therapy. I just can't move. I don't know what's wrong with me," she sobs and grabs at another tissue. The remnants of nearly a whole box of tissues lay scattered on her bed.

She recounts the story of her illness. Now she's at rehab, ready to strengthen her body, and she feels paralyzed. "I can't do it!" I sit with her in silence for a few minutes, just nodding as she relates her frustration.

"What emotion is filling you up right now?" I ask.

She stares at me, does a sharp intake of breath, and exclaims: "Why, it's fear! I'm afraid! I'm afraid to get up!" She looks at me in shocked silence and then exclaims, "I don't have to be afraid. I can do this!"

And sure enough, just recognizing and naming fear is enough to help her move through it. It is a turning point for her. Miriam Greenspan writes that "it's fear of *feeling* fear that stops you. If you can feel it, you can heal it." This was exactly the ailment of the patient above. Greenspan goes on to say that "the raw emotion of fear itself is actually not paralyzing but energizing. Fear moves us to act—and if we avoid instead, the fear only grows."[76]

We need to listen to it. Affirm it. Assess it. Reframe it. Psychologists call reframing feelings "cognitive restructuring." For instance, thinking "I'm weak" when we feel sad or scared can be reframed as "I'm strong and courageous enough to let myself feel sad or scared." Here are a few ways to process this:

- If fear didn't scare me, I would use it to....
- The resources and strengths I now have to use my fears creatively are....
- When I view fear as teacher, I learn....
- Something productive I can do with my fear is....[77]

Contextualize it. Is this a fear for now or part of a story from another time that is influencing the present? When fear can be seen as part of a larger human story, compassion for self and others will come and is a lasting gift. Offer mindfulness or meditative practice or prayer. It is a great tool to help focus and find equanimity. Like the patient above, fear didn't have to stop her. We can all learn how to move through it.

The Buddha says, "If you don't understand the nature of fear, you will never find fearlessness." Since nothing is absolutely determined, there is not only reason to fear but also reason to hope.

"Finding the core of our fear, we find our way."[78] Hope is a ballast that keeps us steady. It recognizes where along the path are the dangers and pitfalls that can throw us off. Hope incorporates fear into the process of rational deliberation and tempers it so we can think and choose without panic.

Another deterrent to hope is despair, "a more complex emotion than either grief or fear."[79] "To despair means to lose all hope; to feel empty and desolate, adrift in a lonely sea, to exist without a sense of purpose or faith, to be disconnected from the flow of life, exiled from a universe of meaning."[80] It is "a complex emotion that contains core elements of grief, anger, and helplessness."[81] "Despair's journey is both a search for renewed meaning and a call to grieve our losses."[82]

I visit a patient who had a cancerous brain tumor removed and suffered a stroke during that surgery.

I enter the room and see the patient curled up on her side in the bed, knees as high as she can get them, a big seam across the top of her head, covers pulled up tight, and skin gray/white. Her husband sits on the nearby couch.

"You called for a chaplain?" I inquire. They both nod yes. I pull up a chair beside her bed, and she begins her story, murmuring in a very quiet, weak voice. "I have been praying and praying and God doesn't answer me. I feel like I'm all alone in the dark. I can't make any progress. I wonder if God is punishing me for something? I don't feel God's presence at all. I am all alone...." She trails off.

I ask about family and friends. She has those. Yes, they are praying for her. Her husband interjects to encourage her, but she ignores him. She says it is one step forward and three steps back. She's losing ground and she just doesn't have the strength to go on. She looks toward the corner of the room while she answers me. Her thoughts are very much turned inward.

"It's really dark for you, isn't it?" I ask. "You must feel very afraid?" She nods. We sit silently. What to do or say here?

"Would it be OK if I read from the Psalms?" She nods. "You know there were a lot of people that felt just like you, and they put their own words to it. Here are a few verses from Psalm 77 (NRSVCE): 'I cry aloud to God, that he may hear me. In the day of my trouble I seek the Lord; in the night my hand is stretched out without wearying; my soul refuses to be comforted. I think of God, and I moan; I meditate, and my spirit faints.'" I look at her and she is watching me now, listening. "When bad things happen to us, and suffering comes, this is how we feel. You are not alone in that," I observe quietly.

We sit there, silent for a long while. I feel a great sadness at what she describes. I've been in the dark pit. I know what that is like. I feel like I'm sitting in there now with her. It almost feels like a physical ache to me. And I don't know how to comfort her. Who knows how long she will stay here, or how hope will come or even if? She's from a traditional Christian background, so I offer to pray for her, and she readily agrees to that. I invite her husband to join hands with us as I pray. I take her stroke-paralyzed left hand in mine. It is cold and limp. If only there were instant medicine for this!

I offer to come back later in the afternoon and give her a session of "healing touch." She nods her assent. And so, about 4:00, I return to the room. This time she's alone, lying on her back, eyes closed. "I'm here to do healing touch with you." She nods, but never opens her eyes, the whole half hour. Three times she murmurs, "Thank you."

I leave and take her situation home with me. All evening long and first thing in the morning, she is heavily on my mind. I decide to pop in before my first meeting of the day to see how she fared during the night.

She's sitting up in bed, having breakfast. She spots me, and exclaims, "Chaplain, I am a lot better!" I am stunned. But indeed, over the next few days, she attacks her physical therapy with new vigor. I see her at therapy, in harness, on the treadmill. "OK, five more of those kicks with your leg. One...two....three...." We all cheer as she works hard to finish well.

I realize that the new spiritual and emotional strength has transferred into her determination to rally her physical self. On Friday, I check in on her. She's on the phone with her sister. "I have to go," she announces. She hangs up and turns to me.

"Chaplain, I need some words on my wall," she says firmly. "What words do you want? I respond. "I can print them off and bring them up." "I need *hope*, *courage*, and *faith* up there." She points across the room. This from the woman who Monday could not have even formed the word *hope* with her lips.

I print the signs, and her husband hangs them up for her. She has one more week with us, and in that week she works very hard at her physical therapy. And on her last day, she leaves walking on her own, with a walker, even talking about returning to work.

What happened here? This was a patient not only paralyzed by fear but also completely gripped by despair. In that first visit, her eyes were all that moved as she watched me. As chaplain, I made space for her to put words to her fear, hopelessness, and grief. I affirmed her truth, not only what she was feeling but also what she knew about her faith. Story and community through the chaplain intervention somehow allowed the light to come in, hope to generate, and healing to begin. There will likely be more setbacks. Although now she knows something she did not know before: there is a way out of the darkness, light will come, and she has within her the power the ability to choose life. Groopman affirms the idea of choice as being paramount to hatching hope. He says,

> Hope can arrive only when you recognize that there are real options and that you have genuine choices. Hope can flourish only when you believe that what you do can make a difference, that your actions can bring a future different from the present. To have hope, then, is to acquire a belief in your ability to have some control over your circumstances. You are no longer entirely at the mercy of forces outside yourself.[83]

Hope generates in many ways. "It can be imagined as a domino effect, a chain reaction, each increment making the next increase more feasible."[84] Physical improvement will definitely grow hope. But even when that cannot occur, we can facilitate hope that positively affects our whole being and even sometimes our family and friends. As we move forward, reframing, practicing gratitude, and settling into new ways of relating to the world hope allows an openness to change, permission to dream a new future, and initiative to set the goals to get there—which brings us to tool 4, Creativity.

6

LEARNING TO DREAM

> Illness was no doubt the final cause of the whole urge to create. By creating, I could recover; by creating I became healthy.
>
> Heinrich Heine, German poet[85]

"Creativity is not a rare ability, but a fundamental aspect of being human," says Rick Rubin, noted record producer, in his book *The Creative Act: A Way of Being*.[86] You might think, "Well, easy for him to say!" But it's true. Reading a book, viewing a landscape, taking a shower, talking with friends, going to a museum...almost all of our activities in life can open us to new ideas, insight, and healing if we are receptive. Inspiration is everywhere. Jim Rendon, in his book on post-traumatic growth, asserts, "Openness to new experience is the personality trait most predictive of creativity."[87] This gift is crucial to moving through the change and journey of transition that trauma has imposed on us.

William Bridges writes that there are three functions of transition. First is *reorientation*. Life has changed and we will have to adjust to the change. The second is that we have a chance for *personal growth* and greater authenticity. Think of the transitions of Moses, forty years herding sheep, and then forty years leading the Israelites. Or Jesus with his forty days in the wilderness before he embraces his ministry. Or Buddha, whose exposure to suffering led him to great wisdom. Or Odysseus, king of Ithaca, and his journey home after the Trojan War. Or your own transitions, perhaps to college, or career, or marriage. Whether short or long, chosen or unchosen, there is something epic in every one of our transitions. Each one has the potential for growth. That's what makes the third function of transition so important. It "gives us access to the wellsprings of our own *creativity*."[88] That ability to find a new solution to a problem, a new method of being, doing, thinking, and expressing yourself, will foster openness to change, a personality trait that is essential to a new future. And science tells us that even the *experience* of the trauma can enhance creativity! This tool will come to bear all along the transition that takes place after trauma.

Unpredictable, challenging, disorienting, downright scary and painful, any one of us tidal waved by trauma and impacted by change has a crucially important transition ahead of them. Life as we know it ends. T. S. Eliot wrote, "The end is where we start from."[89] We enter a liminality, a place between the now and the not yet, where transformation and potential transcendence begin to germinate. Jeff Manion in *The Land Between* observes that this time between an ending and a new beginning "provides the space for God to do some of his deepest work. God intends for us to emerge from this land radically reshaped. But while offering a greenhouse for growth, the Land Between can also be a desert where faith goes to die. Your response determines the end of this journey."[90] Margaret Silf writes: "Transitions are gaps. They mark the gap between the 'no longer' and the 'not yet.' They are the space where we are neither in one place nor another, the hiatus between everything we thought we knew and all that lies ahead in the unknowable future. They mark the place where a certain order breaks down and chaos arrives."[91] She's right about the chaos—emotionally, spiritually, physically, everything is up for grabs. Trauma shatters *everything*. Entering the chaos is where everything is lost and found. There is separation, death, rebirth, decay, renewal, growth, and harvest. It's all in there, and it is terrifying. This liminal space, between trauma and recovery, between endings and beginnings, is the start of a journey.

The many-layered path has some markers along the way. Bridges notes the stages as Ending, Neutral Zone, and New Beginning and that they "are simply the necessary times during which we can incorporate and consolidate the discoveries made and the power released in the transitions."[92]

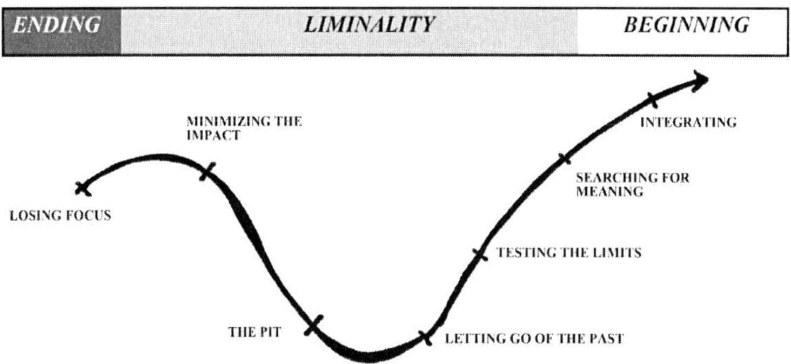

There are many versions of the change curve first developed by Elizabeth Kubler Ross and further expanded by Sabina Spencer and John Adams in *Life Changes*, their book on personal growth.

All have several things in common. Notice that the curve goes down before it goes up. And notice, too, that the new beginning is higher and broader than where you started.

One patient who looked at the map brightened up and said, "Oh, it is so encouraging to know that I will move through this." Others will know exactly where their "red dot" is on the curve. Change, whether chosen or unchosen, whether deep or shallow, and the movement of the transition curve holds true to human experience. It is important to note that for most of us, even without trauma, change is happening all the time. Think of the changes we experienced during the pandemic. It altered the way we traveled to work, the way we did our work, the way we lived at home, the way we shopped, worshipped, received healthcare...the list goes on, and every divergence initiated a new line of transition and adjustment. Remember that "one person's transition can put everyone within a family (or any other human system that the individual belongs to) into transition, too."[93] You as the caregiver are not immune to the stress of your own changes, transitions, and losses. Your attention to self-care is crucial to prevent burnout and exhaustion as you give wholeheartedly to others. Paying attention to the layers of stress generated by change matters to your well-being.

Initially after trauma, there's a *loss of focus*:[94] making plans or concentrating for very long is extremely difficult. Clear thinking eludes us. Absorbing and acknowledging the new reality takes time. Sometimes we try to *minimize the impact*.[95] We try to go backward, to somehow hang on to the life that was before the trauma. But change is constant. The only way through is forward. Letting go of life as we knew it is hard and painful work. "To an extent that we seldom realize, we come to identify ourselves with the circumstances of our lives."[96] When life as we know it ends, the part of us that is defined by roles and relationships, our whole way of being, must redevelop and adjust to a new life pattern. Continuing to exist is a terror. Fear is underneath everything. Underneath for all of us lurks the question: "How will I survive? How will I go on?"

The pit,[97] the wilderness, the land between can be a lonely, dark place, at least at first. The severity of deeply wounding trauma will dictate how long you stay. The letting go, truth telling, attention to feelings, and grieving all take place here, and they happen without light ahead to guide or maybe even any cause for hope. People will begin to come to terms here with the changes in their lives. Endings bring *disengagement*, a forced letting go of the way things were. *Disenchantment* comes with forced acknowledgment and acceptance of new realities and loss of security. William Bridges observed after the painful death of his wife: "If it is deep and far-reaching, transition makes a person feel that not only is a piece of reality gone, but that everything that had seemed to be reality was simply an enchantment. With the spell broken, life can look so different that we hardly recognize it."[98] *Disorientation* between identities reigns, with its loss of rhythm and place in life. But it is disorientation giving way to *reorientation* that will begin to provide a way up and out. Creative opportunity comes out of the chaos.

This stage is where the chaplain or the caregiver can do great work, and this is likely where you will encounter your patients. Helping someone to add to their story, fitting this into their life timeline, accommodating the search for meaning, and counting the losses. This is caregiving work...all held in encouraging, loving, and nonjudgmental, compassionate listening.

Even though Bridges made a chart of transition, he observes that "the neutral zone is never a place on a map. It's inside the mirror or down the rabbit hole or just through the back of the wardrobe. It's light-years away, and it is no farther away than your thumb. It's not a geographical place, but rather a whole new dimension to experience."[99] There is a lot of back-and-forthing in this time between. For the person navigating transition, there will be a time to *do*, but not now. Now it is time to *be*. This liminal pressure cooker will begin the work of healing. This is the time to begin to explore and express those feelings of sadness, anger, and grief. There will be a growing sense of powerlessness and maybe depression. Fear and anger threaten to overwhelm. There may be attitudes and behaviors that are no longer supportive. It is time for kindness, a time to find and receive love and compassion—from others and for the person to give to themselves. It may also be a time for life review, forgiveness, gratefulness, or the completion of unfinished business, which is often the case when we move toward death.

Centuries of human experience tell us the only way through is forward. What will going forward *differently* look like? And how exactly does creativity begin to empower the transformation that can come out of this very intense cauldron of suffering?

The urge to create and imagine is deeply embedded in us. It is interesting to note that Tibetans have no word for creativity. For them, the closest translation is "natural." To be human is to be creative. Musician Michael Card notes that "we are driven to create at this deep wordless level of the soul because we are all fashioned in the image of a God who is an Artist. When we first encounter God in the Bible, it is not as the awesome Lawgiver or the Judge of the universe but as the Artist."[100] This understanding also challenges the widespread misconception that only some of us are blessed with the creative muse. "Creativity springs from all of us, in one way or another," David Benner, professor of psychology and spirituality, and spiritual guide, notes. "We tend to think of creativity only in certain limited spheres of life—the arts, for example—and fail to see that any act that emerges with authenticity from a deep place of spirit and soul is a creative one."[101] Courage and hope gained from community allow us to begin to make adjustments that initially come at great cost. It gives us moments to practice acting freely, which can then act as seeds, enabling a shift from the entrapment of trauma. It is in this liminal space where creativity and openness to change work together to reactualize freedom. Repressed by trauma, fostered by hope, creative activities can ignite innovative thinking necessary to move forward. It sees possibilities and imagines solutions. Creativity can take many forms. Activities like art, music, storytelling, being in nature, participating in a small group, aromatherapy, yoga, practicing mindfulness or prayer all engage our minds, spirits, *and* bodies in actions that require imagining something new or different, a necessary step toward freedom and out of passive, paralyzed bondage.

In the following patient encounter, I used mindfulness meditation (recalling the patient to be aware of herself) by reflecting on a psalm and encouraged deep breathing to help her extreme agitation. Our encounter opened a new way for her to cope with her mother's imminent death in another hospital.

Paged to a room today: "Patient upset! Please come." I am able to respond right away. There is no question about what room she is in. I can hear sobbing and wailing as I walk down the hall.. She's sitting on the side of the bed, rosary in hand, going through the beads as fast as she can, "Hail, Mary, full of grace...." Hardly stopping to breathe, choking on her sobs and the words, she recites the words as tears run down her face. I stand for a few minutes watching her, waiting for her to stop. Tears are important. Whatever is wrong, she needs to grieve it. Finally, I interrupt and introduce myself. She grabs my hand and kisses it and says, "My mom is dying right now in _____ Hospital." Then she turns away, a new burst of tears. She starts in on the prayers again, as fast as she can say them.

The phone rings. She yells into the phone: "My mom is dying right now. Pray for her! I'm talking to the priest!" and slams the phone down. Again, on to the Hail Marys. As she comes to the Lord's Prayer, I say it with her, slowing her down a bit. I wait for another torrent of Hail Marys...and then we repeat the Lord's Prayer together again.

She picks up the phone and dials her sister. "I need mom's phone number beside her bed! I need them to put the phone by her ear so I can read some prayers to her!" As she repeats the phone number, I copy it off for her. Then she grabs for some printed prayers, again speeding through them, her words tumbling over one another. There is no sign of the agitation diminishing, so I finally interrupt again.

"Your mother is dying. I'm so sorry to hear that. You must be very upset. But I wonder if you are hearing what these prayers are saying about God and your mother? You are reading all these prayers very fast...but are you understanding that Mary and Jesus are taking your mother right into God's loving arms?" She halts, listening to me and says, "Oh, I know I should be joyful about that."

"No, that's not what I meant. Your mother is making a transition. But she is going to a place where she will be loved more than she ever has before. Do you believe that?" She nodded.

"I understand that this is a devastating time for you. You are losing your mom. It must be very hard for you. But saying all these prayers so fast doesn't seem to be comforting you very much. Could I ask why you are here in the hospital?"

"I have blood clots. And if I get too upset, I could die at any moment!" She looked at me with new terror in her eyes, aware for the first time of her own agitation.

"Well, then, you need to take care of yourself too, don't you? How about if you lie back on the bed and pay attention to your breathing. See if you can slow that down a bit. I'll read the twenty-third psalm to you. I want you to think about what God is saying to you and your mom in this psalm, OK?" She nods, scoots back onto the bed, puts her feet up. "Breathe...give me another deep breath...breathe." I read it to her very slowly. She tries to cooperate, breathing deeper, and the tears begin to slow.

"Alice [not her real name], God knows what is happening to you and how painful it is. God is also waiting and ready for your mom. And...God is here with you right now."

"Yes," she sniffles, "I understand."

During this time, someone comes in who needs to talk to her about a blood procedure. He says it is urgent but agrees to wait until I finish reading to her. She invites him to sit nearby until we are done.

I say to her, "Alice, I'll come back in a while after your consultation."

"Do you promise?" she asked.

"Yes, I'll come back in an hour or less."

"Oh, thank you, chaplain, please come back."

So I leave, thinking and praying for her.

When I come into the room an hour later, she is dressed. Now she has taken on an entirely different demeanor. "How is your mom?" I ask.

"She's still alive, and my sister is coming to get me. I'm going to the other hospital to see her."

"If your mom was sitting beside you on this bed instead of me, what do you think she would say to you?" I ask, pointing at the bed where we had sat together. She looks at me, mouth open and silent for a moment. After a pause, she says, "She would say, 'Everything is going to be alright!' She would say, 'Take care of yourself. I'm going to be fine and so are you. I'm going to God.'" All this comes out in a rush. She continues to look at me with a stunned expression.

"Well, that's your message then, isn't it?" I ask. "As you go to the hospital, that's the message for you and for her in her journey to God. You hold that message and comfort her with that, OK? Can she speak?"

"No, she can't, but I think she can hear us," she says.

I nod. "I'm sure she can hear you, even if her eyes are closed. You know what to say now, don't you?"

She nods. "I never would have thought of that!" she says. Again, she repeats, "I never would have thought of that! Thank you, chaplain!" I reassure her that I will be praying for her and thinking about her and say goodbye.

The invitation to creative thinking and imagining helped this patient move forward from her extreme anxiety. Imagination fuels empowerment for choice and growth. At its simplest, creativity opens the door to deeply experiencing our true selves.

In the following patient encounter, an invitation to "imagine" leads to reassurance and peace:

I come into a two-patient room to welcome the new patient and do assessment on spiritual needs. She tells me she's Catholic in background and seems receptive to attending Mass, which we offer once a week, and to receiving visits from a communion minister. As we talk, she says, "Chaplain, I'm just so anxious! I can't sleep. I can't pray. I just can't settle down at all...can you help me?" "Have you ever done guided imagery meditation?" I ask. She shakes her head no, but says, "I'd like to try it." Her roommate is Muslim, and she chimes in from the other side of the room. "I want to do it, too! Can I do it, too?" So we gather together, one in the bed and one in a wheelchair. I turn on the sound of ocean waves and encourage them to breathe deeply, to do a body scan, to feel where they might be holding tension. And I invite them into the story in Mark's Gospel where Jesus feeds five thousand people on the hillside.

"You can see the scene: the multitudes, the hillside, the rocks, warm sunshine, the sea in the background...and Jesus is there. You hear the sounds all around: the chatter of children, the soft breeze blowing across the grasses, a baby crying in her mother's arms, most of all the embracing voice of Jesus himself. You smell the water, the air....You are close enough to hear Jesus's calming voice....How wonderful to sit here and let his words wash over you. All afternoon, you sit and listen....And evening begins to come. You realize that you are hungry...everyone is. It has been a wonderful afternoon. But now what? You are sitting close enough that you get to see a discussion with the disciples. They're concerned about the people. And one boy comes up with a basket. Five loaves and two fishes...what can Jesus do with that? It's not enough! You can see his disciples are doubting, too. Jesus gives thanks, and one by one people line up. You get in the line, too. Everyone dips into the basket and comes out with food. What kind of thing is this? You are experiencing a miracle. And there are leftovers, even! Think of the abundance! You've just had an experience of how God loves people.

"Finally, the multitudes disperse. You are alone now. It's been quite a day. You sit on a rock overlooking the water lapping up on the shore. You listen to the waves. In your mind you rehearse all that has just transpired. You are quiet. Then Jesus walks up and sits on the rock beside you. Together you are quiet for a time. Then Jesus speaks: 'What can I do for you?' he asks. The question shoots deep....And you tell him [I wait in silence for a minute]... whatever is in your heart.

"You receive his healing and blessing. Once again you are still, sitting there together. Finally, you turn and ask the Master, 'What can I do for you?' And you listen....

I give them some time and then bring them out of the meditation by stretching. They open their eyes. "So...did Jesus have anything to say to you?" (I never know if an invitation like this and a first-time guided imagery will work.) But the first patient says, "Yes! Jesus told me to relax. I'm going to be OK. I don't need to worry about everything!" And the second patient says, "He talked to me, too! I'm going to be fine. I just need to do the therapies. I feel so much better!"

The women talk excitedly together as I take my leave. Our hospital offers many kinds of therapies that will help them be open to whatever is ahead for them. They've just experienced a creative way to not only touch into their faith, but to calm their fear and anxiety. They have new assurance for going forward.

Daily work often provides some structure and connection when we are in the chaos. Our hospital understands this. Every morning the patient is given a schedule of his day, which can include several sessions of physical, occupational, and speech language therapies. Other options are offered around these scheduled times: art, music, dance, drama, an escort to the park or to the lakefront for a nature walk. Any medium that can help bring new perspective and enlarge a patient's world assists in improving physical health, reducing hospital stays, and generally enhancing quality of life. Jim Rendon, the journalist who researched and wrote about post-traumatic growth, says these interventions work because "that absorption, or flow, an intense concentration that merges both action and awareness...can produce a sense of competence and accomplishment, and positive emotion....It helps inspire people to find more creative ways to address their problems"[102] and assists the move through the land between.

As we work to find creative new approaches to old situations, there's always the temptation to stick to old patterns. But openness to change matters. A study that explored the relationship between self-reported post-traumatic growth and creativity, authored by Marie Forgeard, indicated that "the higher people were in openness to new experiences, the more creative growth they reported."[103] Creativity begins to foster growth in other areas of life, imagining new ways to reorient, re-enchant, and reidentify. Creativity also generates self-efficacy, which "is the way we perceive ourselves and our belief that the things we do make a difference."[104]

Our value system, challenged at the onset of the trauma, begins to grow resilient as values, meaning, and purpose are reconstructed. There's no bounce back to what was, but a way forward opens as a new future is imagined and improvised. Armed with resilience, we will aim for progress. We will have the patience and strength to appreciate the "yet" of our recovery. "Adversity is a catalyst for new ways of seeing, understanding, and creating." Henri Matisse said, "Only what I created after my illness constitutes my real self."[105]

Martin Buber, Jewish philosopher, theologian, storyteller, and wise teacher wrote:

> I do not accept any absolute formulas for living. No preconceived code can see ahead to everything that can happen in a man's life. As we live, we grow, and our beliefs change. They must change. So I think we should live with this constant discovery. We should be open to this adventure in heightened awareness of living. We should stake our whole existence on our willingness to explore and experience.[106]

We begin to move forward when we are ready. For those who have experienced severe trauma, it could be a long time. On Bridges's map, the next step is "*looking forward to the future.*" Spencer and Adams refer to it *as letting go of the past.*[107] *Revolution begins.* "Reorientation, personal growth, authentication and creativity all require that you let go of the way that you have experienced yourself."[108] The question is not "Why did this happen to me?" but now becomes "How am I going to go on?" It's time to be gentle with yourself. Hope and creativity, which feed each other, begin to build a new sense of self—and eventually, a new self-confidence. As one survivor said, "The trauma didn't define me—it refined me in a painful process of growth to become a better person than I ever could have been otherwise."[109]

The next stage, according to Spencer and Adams, is "*testing the limits of a new life.*" There's new energy and enthusiasm. We begin to actively look for ways to test ourselves in our new situation. New identities, new skills, and a new sense of confidence are being established. We have survived! This is the time to make sure there is community that offers the love and support that is so needed.

The *search for meaning* intensifies. There's a shift in our energy from being very active and involved to spending more time alone, reflecting on the experience, trying to understand. Mindfulness, meditation, and prayer work particularly well at this stage. There are "treasures" to uncover beyond the curve. Comparing experiences with others who have begun the same adjustments is helpful. It's time to share gained experience and wisdom. Opportunity will come in understanding how change and transition have helped spur growth and understanding of deeper meanings in life. Transformation is at hand.

The final step of transition comes with the *integration* of discoveries and experiences into everyday life. Patients stay at our hospital anywhere from two weeks to six months or more. But it is unlikely that chaplains get to witness this part of the path through transition. Sometimes patients come back to say "thank you" and tell you more about their reentry into life. If you are ministering in a community rather than a hospital, you may have the privilege of accompanying the way forward into new territory. Spiritual care offers tremendous opportunity to help people along this road. There will be flashbacks and waves of grief. Learning new things is possible. Focus can happen. The process shouldn't be hurried. Making sense of the experience might take a lifetime. The process can bring peace and strength. We have found new ways to cope and move forward. There's a new sense of the preciousness of life, the importance of relationships, and likely a renewed sense of purpose. The openness to change engendered by interventions of creativity will renew faith shaken or shattered in trauma. Transcendence begins.

7

CHOOSING FAITH

> Faith is the word that describes the direction our feet start moving when we find that we are loved. Faith is stepping out into the unknown with nothing to guide us but a hand just beyond our grasp.
>
> Frederick Buechner[110]

People interviewed in the aftermath of trauma reported that faith was one of the tools that helped them recover. What is faith? There are probably as many definitions as the people who claim it. It is mysterious and hard to define. Abraham Heschel calls faith more than a religious tradition:

> It is a creative situation, an event. For God is not always silent, and man is not always blind. In every man's life there are moments when there is a lifting of the veil at the horizon of the known, opening a sight of the eternal. Each of us has at least once in his life experienced the momentous reality of God....The remembrance of that experience and the loyalty to the response of that moment are the forces that sustain our faith. In this sense, *faith is faithfulness*, loyalty to an event, loyalty to our response.[111]

Faith is a doorway to what is beyond us, and the pathway to transcendence. Madeleine L'Engle calls it "that which lies on the *other* side of reason. Faith is what makes life bearable, with all its tragedies and ambiguities and sudden, startling joys."[112]

Spirituality and religion both play a role in faith. Kenneth Pargament, a psychology professor at Bowling Green State University in Ohio, spent his career considering the role that faith plays in trauma recovery and growth. He says that being religious can be helpful both when it comes to healing from trauma and when it comes to growth. "When religious people suffer a traumatic event, they can place their suffering in a larger context. Faith can give their suffering a deeper meaning or purpose, another framework to explain their experience."[113]

But he also observed that spiritual engagement, regardless of religious tradition, helps people find positive ways to cope and grow. For those who are spiritual and not religious, it may be helpful to tap into the sacredness of life. "If people can identify things that have the deepest meaning and then work to better incorporate them into their lives, they are more likely to heal from trauma and change for the better....It can be anything, a loving relationship, work, the environment, making the world a better place."[114] In whatever way you want to think about spirituality, we may confidently assert that everyone has some form of it.[115]

A 2023 article in the *New York Times* explored the idea that "many people are experiencing painful moves away from the religions in which they were raised. Additionally, there seemed to be a consensus among the readers...that there isn't a lot of room in a secular society to express faith outside of traditional houses of worship." And yet, the writer also observed that "the one thing most secular organizations and clubs have been unable to quite replicate in the United States: a ready-made, supportive community that brings together people from different ages and walks of life...in a time of rapid religious change...where we will see new forms of spirituality and community take root."[116] We are definitely in a time where traditions, religious practices, beliefs, and faith are being questioned, redefined, or in some cases cast aside. Whether you are spiritual, religious, or a "None," faith is still named by those who have recovered from trauma as the fifth tool in this ascending spiral to transcendence. How is this power such a source of strength for moving forward despite all obstacles?

The Bible often speaks of the power of faith and belief. But perhaps they have slightly different functions even though both are necessary to meaning-making. Belief refers to what experience or reason has taught us. (You will recall that belief is a strong contributor to hope.) Belief shines a light on understanding. Belief, based on knowledge and experience gathered from the past, rests more in the left brain's analytic judging area. It accumulates "facts." Will beliefs change with trauma? Absolutely. It does not have the power for transformation that faith has. But it is choosing to believe that brings the gift and power of faith. "Faith," as Frederick Buechner notes, "is better understood as a verb than a noun, as a process than as a possession. It is on-again-off-again rather than once-and-for-all. Faith is not being sure where you're going but going anyway. A journey without maps."[117] Faith is the walk in the dark.

Faith can also be misunderstood as conviction in beliefs. Professor Shane Clifton, dean of theology in Sydney, Australia, involved in an accident that left him a quadriplegic, observed: "We tend to have faith as the belief that God will heal you. A belief that you'll be able to experience some sort of perfect psychological and physical health. Whereas faith is trust in God *whatever* the circumstances. The object of faith isn't healing or psychological health. The object of faith should be God."[118]

In the Christian tradition, Richard Rohr, an American Franciscan priest and writer on spirituality, defines it as "a foundational belief that life is a succession of dyings and risings. At the center of the Eucharist, we proclaim, 'Christ has died, Christ is risen, and Christ will come again.' That is the saving pattern! It is not *a* mystery of faith; it is *the* mystery of faith."[119] Faith, like belief, which can be shattered by traumatic experiences, rests in the heart, or right brain, and is a force given to us to move beyond ourselves, to transcend the trauma that has wreaked havoc, and to move forward toward hope and healing. Our experiences inform our faith and expand our beliefs. A redefined faith after trauma can be life changing. For all of us who have undergone trauma, are experiencing loss, and are moving through transition, reclaiming and reforming a faith that accommodates the journey of suffering and dying and rising to new life is crucial to recovery.

Chaplains are guardians, protectors, and facilitators of patients' spirituality. We begin with assessment. The loss of faith and belief due to trauma is sometimes termed "spiritual distress." As defined by Betty Ferrell and Christina Puchalski in their book *Making Health Care Whole*, it refers to a person's "impaired ability to experience and integrate meaning and purpose in life through connectedness with self, other, art, music, literature, nature, and/or power greater than oneself."[120] Signs include feelings of anger or hopelessness, feeling abandoned or betrayed by God, questioning or having doubts about one's held spiritual/religious beliefs, or asking "why?" in the search for meaning. We are most effective with others when we can accurately identify problem areas and needs in the spiritual lives of our patients and there are many assessment tools available to help us.[121]

We ask: What are your sources of support? How do you find meaning in your situation? Is there a cultural background or faith that supports you? We evaluate: What is lost? What are the adjustments? What do you need? We go to our toolboxes for specific interventions that will help the patient put words to what has happened, to begin the process of grieving, and to start the journey toward accommodating change and redefining faith. We encourage storytelling, provide loving, listening presence, help to grow hope by setting goals and adjusting to new truths. However, there is a personal choosing to faith. While this gift comes from outside of us, it requires an openness to receiving it. This is where the creative interventions mentioned in the last chapter may provide new ways of thinking, new ways of understanding who God is, and making sense of our journeys. This gift comes from outside *and* inside. And it often involves the struggle of doubt.

As spiritual caregivers, we do our deepest work here. Permission to doubt may be your first gift to another as they process what's happened to them. Faith that starts by doubting existing belief systems may birth a new faith, a new kind of generative faith that loves and sees in bigger, broader ways. The beginning of faith is doubt, not the sureness of beliefs. Francis Bacon writes in *DeAugmentis*: "If we begin with certainties, we will end in doubt. But if we begin with doubts and bear them patiently, we may end in certainty."[122] Zen practice affirms: "The greater the doubt, the greater the awakening; the smaller the doubt, the smaller the awakening. No doubt, no awakening."[123] As Brian McLaren wrote: "There is faith after doubt, and life after doubt, and life with doubt. If you thought life before doubt was good, wait until you see where doubt can lead you and what doubt can teach you. You don't have to feel ashamed or be afraid."[124]

Faith holds tremendous potential for love, hope, community, and transformation. It is more than an emotion. It is a whole-body experience that invites action and opens the way to transcendence. We think of transcendence as the way to rise above, to soar. And yet transcendence is also a grounding outside of ourselves. A good example of faith at work is in the movie *Indiana Jones and the Last Crusade*.[125] Indiana Jones is at the edge of a deep chasm. He is under severe pressure to get to the other side. There is no way. Desperate, he consults his notes, murmurs, "It's a leap of faith," takes a deep breath, puts his hand over his heart, and steps out into thin air, only for a bridge, hidden by an optical illusion, to suddenly appear under his feet. He takes another wobbly step and ends up running across the gorge to safety. Faith is like that. It encompasses all of us, not just our minds. We hold it. We act out of it. We connect to God through it. It is noun and verb. Liel Libovitz, Israeli journalist and author, writes:

> As any committed believer will tell you, faith isn't just felt; it must be practiced. To live a life of observance is to strive to embody the principles passed on to us from on high in deed rather than just in word. That's why Catholics tithe and fast and attend Mass, why Muslims make the hajj to Mecca, why Jews observe the Sabbath and abstain from eating pork. Take away the actions, and you're left with atomized ideas floating in the ether, which is an enervating condition.[126]

When Jesus says, "For truly I tell you, if you have faith the size of a mustard seed, you will say to this mountain, 'Move from here to there,' and it will move; and nothing will be impossible for you" (Matt 17:20), he is talking about the kind of power that somehow rests outside of ourselves and yet is accessible to us.

The Christian tradition teaches that faith is a gift of God and provides the power for being and doing. And the mystery of faith is that while it is gift, our own strength joins to make a powerful response for life. No wonder it is named as a tool for recovery of trauma! As Peter Marty editorialized in the *Christian Century*, "Understanding our lives as a daily gift is a huge part of discovering faith. To view life as a daily gift means there's a giver behind that gift."[127] Biblical faith is never simply giving assent to a certain set of facts or beliefs. It is trust and commitment that result in a change of behavior, a commitment to something bigger than oneself. Buddhist thought teaches this commitment and trust concept through the term *saddhâ*, which means to give one's heart over to or place one's heart upon something.

In Hebrews 11:1, Paul writes: "Now faith is the assurance of things hoped for, the conviction of things not seen." If you have time, check out that chapter for the stories of faith that empowered and embodied action. Faith lies beyond verification. By faith these people overthrew kingdoms, ruled with justice, and received what God had promised them. Their weakness was turned to strength. Buechner writes that hope sits at the outermost edge and driving power of faith. "To have faith is to remember and wait, and to wait in hope is to have what we hope for already begin to come true in us through our hoping."[128]

Madeleine L'Engle notes that "faith is for that which lies on the other side of reason. Faith is what makes life livable, with all its tragedies and ambiguities and sudden, startling joys."[129] She combines faith and belief:

> In the realm of faith, I KNOW far more than I can believe with my finite mind. I KNOW that a loving God will not abandon what he creates. I KNOW that the human calling is cocreation with this power of love. I KNOW that "neither death, nor life, nor angels, nor principalities, nor powers, nor things present, nor things to come, nor height, nor depth, nor any other creature shall be able to separate us from the love of God, which is in Christ Jesus our Lord.[130]

A patient—I'll call her Carol (not her real name)—found a way to make new meaning of her situation, rediscover her faith, and connect once again with God:

I round the corner of the nurse's station and hear her before I see her...sitting in the doorway of her room, mostly bald from chemo, imperiously yelling orders from her wheelchair to nurses studiously avoiding meeting her eyes. One murmurs to me, "Can't YOU do something with her? She has been like this for all the days she's been in rehab." I can see she's angry. And everyone is tired of her rudeness. It's not their fault she's ill. They are all trying hard to care for her.

"Could we talk a bit in your room?" I ask. She nods, pleased that someone is paying attention. I push her wheelchair back into her room and sit down to chat. She used to be Methodist, she reports. Sang in the choir, was active in her church, taught Sunday school. "But then God left me," she says matter-of-factly.

"God left you? When did that happen?" I ask.

"I don't know, but I'm alone now. Other friends have died and I have no family."

"So you are really alone, aren't you?" I observe. She nods. "Did God leave about the time you got sick?" She nods again, slowly: "Yes, I believe that is right." I can see she is connecting her physical situation with feelings of abandonment.

We visit for quite a while. Eventually, the aide puts her into bed. And I ask, "Would you like me to read you a bedtime story before I go?"

"Yes, that would be nice."

"Do you want something from *Guideposts*, or something from the Bible?"

"I want you to read something from the Bible...you pick it," she says.

So I think to myself, *What story, God? What is the right thing here?* My eyes light on the story of the woman touching the hem of Jesus's garment. "OK, I have a story for you. Sit back and listen."

I read her the story. We discuss the plight of the woman in the story and Jesus's additional healing in bringing this woman back into her community. He saw her. He wanted the crowd to see her. She hasn't been looked at or included as a human being for a long time. We have a good discussion. I see some connections between Carol and the woman in the story. Thank you, God, for helping me pick this story! I say goodnight and leave.

It really bothers me that she thinks God left her. Of course, God's right there and has been there all along. But how to help her see it? How will she recover a lost faith? I pray for her in the night, exercising my own faith.

The next morning, I round the corner again...and for the first time she's *not* talking loudly from her doorway. I step into the room, where the aide is helping her dress for the day. She says "thank you" to the aide! She is being polite and friendly! This is *new*. She catches sight of me and motions me over. "Oh, chaplain, I need to talk to you! You know that story you read me last night?"

I nod.

"I discovered something last night!" She leans back in her chair, a Cheshire smile spreading across her face. I've not seen her smile before. She's really behaving differently this morning.

"What did you discover?" I ask.

"Well, that woman was sick...she'd been sick a long time."

She looks at me for confirmation and I say, "You're right...go on."

"Well, she'd be too weak to fight her way to Jesus through that crowd."

"Yes, maybe so," I venture, wondering where she's going with this.

"Jesus helped her get to him!" she says triumphantly. She waves her finger at me and grins. "Jesus helped her! She couldn't have done that by herself. She was too sick! And I came up with that all by myself in the night," she says proudly, beaming at me.

This discovery changes her. This patient, by herself, with God's Spirit, in the middle of the night, touched Jesus's hem for herself and was called back to life and faith. I don't need to prove that God is present to her. She's found her way. She is a new woman...transformed, excited, changed. Her faith is restored. I celebrate her new understanding of how God is with her. She's loved and she no longer feels alone. It makes all the difference in her attitude to the staff and cooperation with therapy.

How does one retrieve a shattered faith after trauma? As Anne Sexton lamented, "I love faith, but have none."[131] Madeleine L'Engle suggested, it helps to review what you *know*. Like the patient, Carol, it helps to tell the truth about how you feel and where you are. Like the psalmist, it helps to reach out for God, to *remember* what God has done, and to embrace that God is well acquainted with our sorrows. Should we be comforted by the knowledge that Jesus still had scars of his wounding even after resurrection? God is with us. God grieves with us. God loves us. The challenge is to know that in a new and deeper way.

Carol, yearned for what had been lost to her. In a way she was saying, "Yes, God, yes, even though I'm in the pit, and feel alone, I choose you." Research on trauma and spirituality finds that "recovery often requires creating a new sense of one's place in the world and shifts in one's relationships with other people, and possibly with God."[132] God patiently waits for our yes as a part of our healing. It is in that pit of transition, with its invitation to surrender, its confusion, its unknowing that opportunity comes for a bigger, broader, renewed faith.

As we begin to relax into a truly alive, Spirit-filled, dynamic journey of life, we can experience joy, gratefulness, love—all the emotions that are so healing to our bodies and our spirits. Out of this new "being" comes a new "doing" as we understand more about our purpose and find meaning in suffering, life, and death. It is truly the pathway to transformation and transcendence.

A number of studies have found a high correlation between religious faith and growth. One large review of 103 studies of post-traumatic growth found that religious coping was more often correlated with growth than most other attributes including community support or optimism—though those were not too far behind.[133] I would suggest that this is due to the way faith operates within us. Faith provides a framework for who and how we are and the pathway to what is beyond us; it is the "ground of being" coined by Paul Tillich, to describe the intangible and unexplainable presence of God and source of interconnectedness with the world. Whether you are Buddhist, Jewish, Hindu, Christian, or other, these things are true.

Faith is not simply the *last* tool in the row. A faith, newly redefined after trauma, incorporates and informs the post traumatic growth tools of story, community, hope, and creativity within sacred, transcendent space.

Stories grow through exercise of faith, and we understand we are part of a larger story. Life is not just about us. There's something out there, something larger going on that we can connect to. Faith can determine, fuel, and reframe the reflections on life that we put in our stories. Bessel van der Kolk writes: "At the core of recovery is self-awareness."[134] Before the telling comes the story. Before the story comes awareness; before awareness come the feelings. It's a process toward wholeness that starts with recognition of what's deep inside. Faith informs all of this.

Community often takes place within the context of religious practice and ritual, shared beliefs, and life experience. Religious services with practice of worship, prayer together as expression of relationship, and shared support provide opportunity for faith to grow and flourish. Van der Kolk writes: "Restoring relationships and community is central to restoring well-being...language gives us the power to change ourselves and others by communicating our experiences, helping us define what we know, and finding a common sense of meaning."[135]

Hope works very closely together with faith. First Corinthians 13:13 says, "And now faith, hope, and love abide...." What is the distinction, why mention both? Hope is earnest anticipation of true coming events. Faith is the complete trust or confidence in that something. Faith is the bedrock from which hope springs. Rubem Alves, Brazilian poet and philosopher, said, "Hope is the ability to hear the music of the future. Faith is the courage to dance to it today."[136] Jacques Philippe, a priest from the French Community of the Beatitudes, observes: "It could be said that, while charity is the greatest of the three theological virtues, in practice hope is the most important. As long as hope remains, love develops. If hope is extinguished, love grows cold. A world without hope soon becomes a world without love. But hope needs faith, from which it springs."[137]

We all perhaps employ hope in slightly different ways. Buddhists hope for a release from suffering and a way to build a better world. "Faith and hope are the two most prominent characteristics of Judaism,"[138] finding in *tikvah* the hope for a better future, and *tocheles* yearning for a better life that is sure to come. A Hindu appropriates hope in the journey toward enlightenment and spiritual growth. A Muslim maintains hope in the grace and love of Allah, through regular practice of prayer and trust for deliverance in this life and the next. Hope for the Christian is defined as the trusting expectation that God loves, is present to, and promises an ultimate destiny and reunion with Jesus Christ. Encouraging, managing, guiding hope for our diverse patient populations is a cautious process. But what is true is that *all* of us appropriate it in some way. Setting goals and working toward a future reality opens a pathway for the growth of faith.

Creativity can aid the willingness to "see," to consider, to understand, to reimagine in new ways; it can open us to the power of faith, and faith empowers further openness to change. Learning new ways to pray and practice and choose brings courage and strength. It furthers the journey of transformation. Faith and belief challenged and engaged will result in growth, just as Tedeschi and

Calhoun discovered. Old contracts with God are replaced with a new trust that sees God not as deserter or punisher in time of trauma but as compassionate presence. Faith is what ignites the energy to move, allows us to take a risk, opens us to seeing truth for ourselves rather than letting us fall back to old ways. The Bible recounts so many instances of faith at work. Peter's journey to sustaining faith took several tries and stumbles. Remember Peter's confident jump out of the boat? And then trusting his own resources, starts to sink? Madeleine L'Engle, reflecting on Peter's story, suggests, "If we cry out for help (as Peter did), we will be pulled out of the water; we won't drown. And if we listen, we will hear; if we look, we will see."[139]

Post-Traumatic Growth Tools at work...

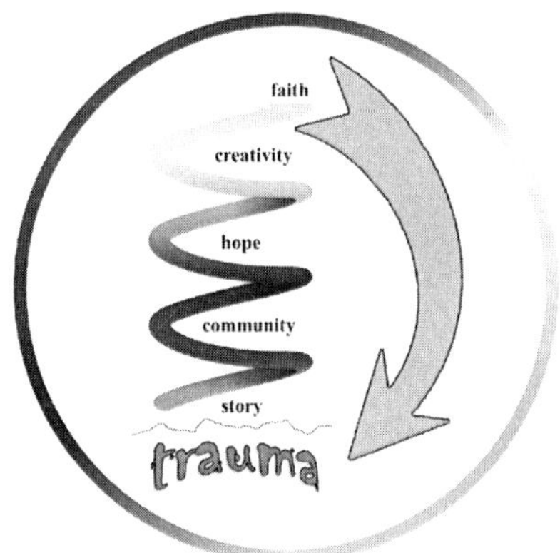

Here's the way these tools work together:

Trauma happens, with its shaking of faith, loss of identity, and broken connections with people and place.

1. Story forms; meaning-making begins.
2. Community listens, shares, and loves.
3. Hope hatches new life.
4. Creativity ignites openness to change.

5. Faith provides meaning and connection. The new, deeper faith, born out of suffering, circles around to inform the person's existing story. And now the story is bigger—the person's story rests within a larger story. Transcendence is at work. Community is engaged at a deeper level...well, all the tools are!

This newly earned wisdom adds hope, connection, and possibility for a now-broader spiritual life. It is like an ascending, expanding circle of connection and relatedness to others and to God that gets deeper and richer as it ascends. Not that this kind of spiritual formation isn't possible for all of us, but somehow, out of suffering and trauma, as we have observed, there is gift and impetus that can take us more quickly along this journey. Positive change can and will come.

Post-traumatic tools and outcomes stream through many of the Biblical stories. In the account of the journey to Emmaus, Luke recounts how Jesus skillfully uses them all to bring transformation to the journeyers.

Imagine for a moment that you are one of the people in Luke's Gospel (24:13–32) walking on the road to Emmaus: wounded, afraid, confused, traumatized by one of the worst things you could possibly have experienced—the crucifixion of your leader Jesus. Hope and future are lost. Who are they now? Where will they go? What will they do? And Jesus, being a good chaplain, somehow unrecognized by them, comes along side and says, "Tell me about it." *He invites their story*, and they begin to pour out their fear, doubts, and trauma to him. He listens compassionately and reviews what they know and what they feel they might have lost about their beliefs and their faith. *He connects them to a bigger story*. The way isn't clear yet. But now they've been drawn beyond themselves. He's listening to them, and they are listening to him.

And the invitation comes..."Stay with us." *Community is about to do what it does best*. There will be further sharing over dinner. They've invited the stranger in...who invited them to community on the road. Henri Nouwen says,

> When the flesh—the lived human experience—becomes word, community can develop. When we say, "Let me tell you what we saw. Come and listen to what we did. Sit down and let me explain to you what happened to us. Wait until you hear whom we met," we call people together and make our lives into lives for others. The word brings us together and calls us into community. When the flesh becomes word, our bodies become part of a body of people.[140]

Hope is not yet in this story. Remember that they spoke of lost hope, misunderstood hope: "We had hoped he was the Messiah who had come to rescue Israel...."

In the embodiment of presence, in the *creativity of ritual*, Jesus breaks the bread and gives thanks. He gives them manna for their wilderness. They are called to remember, to connect, and *their eyes are opened.* There's a new truth and reality, and they see it! *Hope floods in.* Do you see how Jesus is skillfully bringing them to a new understanding, sense of meaning, and restoration of their faith? He invites them to gratefulness. What is one of the first signs of moving through grief? When a person acknowledges the sadness of loss but can be grateful for what was given even though it is now lost. There is a future! They were operating from false assumptions or beliefs about their traumatic experience. And Jesus showed them truth and invited them to transformation and transcendence.

Transformation requires a willingness to challenge your basic beliefs about who you are and *let go* of identities that no longer work for you to move toward healing. Didn't they have to let go of everything they "thought" they knew to find healing? A new vision was required. Jesus delivered it.

They encountered Jesus's transforming presence in and through *his* story and theirs. Sometimes we find our identity and then join the larger identity...sometimes the larger identity helps us discover ours. "Then their eyes were opened, and they recognized him." And they understood something about themselves in the process. Jesus used all the tools to heal and bring these travelers to a *new faith...deeper, wider, broader*, which will inform everything to come.

No longer are they the hopeless, devastated journeyers, retreating to home. "And in that same hour they got up and returned to Jerusalem," this time, full of good news, hope, and transformed faith, eager for relationship with the community they had left behind...all those outcomes we talked about in the beginning of this book:

1. Increased inner strength
2. An openness to new possibilities in life
3. Closer and often deeper relationships with friends and family
4. An enhanced appreciation for life
5. A stronger sense of spirituality

Can we embrace the idea that new, bigger, better life is possible out of suffering? Can we come from the dark pit into flourishing? Think back about the traumas in your own life, and perhaps how these tools have worked to move you forward to the outcomes above—or perhaps how you are still suspended in trauma. It is time to make sure that you welcome and add all these tools to your life.

This prescriptive can provide hope and healing for all including those living lives of ongoing trauma from poverty, gun violence, war, discrimination, and microinsults. One woman wailed to me, "But my trauma is ongoing! I am not 'post-trauma'!" Understanding the impact of loss and the role of lament in story, managing our dark emotions, and giving and receiving love in community, recognizing the path through change and transition, and rebuilding hope and faith will provide support for coping and surviving in the midst of trauma.

These tools are our "manna" in the wilderness. They have the potential to light the way to a life that flourishes despite the layers of stress, ongoing trauma, or even succeeding traumas that come upon us. All of us must say yes to the archetypal journey that trauma invites us to.

Recently, a friend coming out of a relationally traumatic situation, wounded and sore, decided to take a rafting trip with a group of people. She reported to me that she camped and talked and laughed and hiked and jumped off a waterfall. She said the personal connections were meaningful and profound, and many of the group were people of faith who shared their own painful stories and growth processes. They talked about love, suffering, and how to live beautiful lives. She said they even had a wedding one night—complete with vows, music, and dancing—and concluded: "I made a big shift toward growth and healing." All the tools of post-traumatic growth were present in this adventure.

Each step of the way involves challenge and work. Each tool requires acceptance and application. Perhaps, as we work with others, even in community organizing and decidedly nonindividual gestures, the tools can bring healing, growth and positive affect can heal and grow and positively affect communities struggling with racism, poverty, crime, and illness. As individuals find healing, maybe communities will, too.

Think about the grouping of these five tools and how they work together. Think about how the progression leads the journey to recovery. Think about how spiritual formation comes. Think deeply about how you can incorporate this framework of healing into your practice or community, no matter where your ministry is. Think about how you can apply these to yourself. Essential for ministry, and essential for us as well.

For us as caregivers, it is imperative that we have a way to evaluate, notice, and hold our own faith journey. Attention to our own soul care is crucial. We need hope and faith to walk into patient rooms. We need support as we enter people's pain. As we move through the continuing changes and transitions of life, we will learn to negotiate our wounds, find new ways to survive, and absorb new meaning and purpose for our lives as well as those we care for. Deeply held within all spiritualities, biblical, and affirmed by psychologists, this is a pathway for recovery and flourishing.

Amen.

RESOURCES

THE TREE OF LIFE IDENTITY EXERCISE[141]

(*Draw a tree, or print off the outline of a tree with its roots from the internet.*)

The Roots

Write where you come from on the roots. This can be your birthplace, culture, ethnic background, family.

The Ground

Write the things you choose to do on a weekly basis on the ground.

The Trunk

Write your skills and values on the trunk.

The Branches

Write your hopes, dreams, and wishes on the branches. These can be personal, communal, or general.

The Leaves

Write names of those who are significant to you in a positive way. Your friends, family, pets, heroes.

The Fruits

Write the legacies that have been passed on to you.

CIRCLES OF SUPPORT[142]

Chapter 4: "Gathering Support"

Here are some things to think about:[143]

Do you feel a sense of belonging? To others, to yourself?

A circle to which I usually turn for support is...

A circle where I find it difficult to ask for support is...

A time when I expected support from a particular circle and did not get it was...

A time when I got support from a circle that I didn't expect to help was...

The biggest barriers I have to nurturing the center circle, self-intimacy, is...

Is there a new circle I should add?

Is there a circle that isn't working for me?

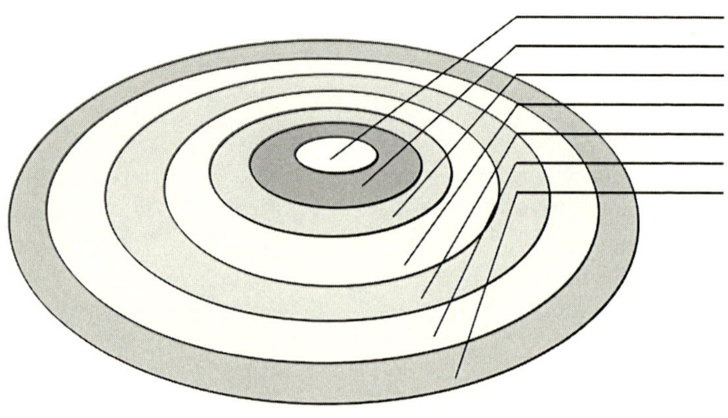

Where am I in my circles?

Where is God in my circles?

RITUAL FOR PHYSICAL LOSS

Props: place a mat or small cloth for patient's tray table, aloe plant, votive candle and matches, CD player with instrumental background music such as Chuck Newman's Quiet Places, and notebook with ritual.

GATHERING

Patient is either in bed or sitting in wheelchair in room. *Do not disturb* sign posted on door. Start music, light candle, read from notebook.

We light this candle to signify the presence of God with us, who is light to our darkness, comfort in our mourning, and healing for our suffering.

TELLING

We meet today to express grief and mourn the loss of your ________ [name whatever the loss is]. You have lost a part of you. The whole sense of your self has been wounded. The losses are many: loss of function, movement, wholeness, integrity, balance. There is pain, not only physical from nerve endings severed and suffering but also from emotional sadness. Bodily image, sensations, and functions once taken for granted have been modified into something new. You cannot escape the reality of this loss. We claim with you the legitimacy of your grief. Can there be relief from this unbearable wound? Can grace fill the space now empty, rendered impotent?

TAKING ACTION

Hear the word of the Lord for you in Lamentations:

My soul continually thinks of it
  and is bowed down within me.
But this I call to mind,
  and therefore I have hope:
The steadfast love of the LORD never ceases,
  his mercies never come to an end;
they are new every morning;
  great is your faithfulness.
"The LORD is my portion," says my soul,
  "therefore I will hope in him." (Lam 3:20–24)

We are created in the image and likeness of God. We come to know God as embodied people. Our hope is in a God who loves us, who became embodied and dwelt among us, and who knows what it is like to have a body, who suffered like we suffer.

___________ [patient name], I invite you to say, "**Lord, hear my prayer**," as we pray together.

Dear God, grant ______________ [patient name]
—comfort to face the devastation of this agonizing loss
...Lord, hear my prayer
—endurance in the face of pain
...Lord, hear my prayer
—protection against disease and infection
...Lord, hear my prayer
—strength and healing for body and spirit
...Lord, hear my prayer
—wisdom to accept what seems unacceptable
...Lord, hear my prayer
—resilience to face change
...Lord, hear my prayer

—peace from your presence

...Lord, hear my prayer

—faith to reclaim life and identity

...Lord, hear my prayer

________________ [patient name], is there anything else that you would like to add? [Allow time for patient to name requests].

Amen.

SENDING

This is an aloe plant. It's a survivor. It tolerates drought, shade, and rough handling. During times of stress, it will become dormant, awaiting favorable conditions to reemerge. It can be uprooted, thrown carelessly on a compost heap, and it will begin to thrive within a short time. It is one of nature's first-aid kits. If you break off one of its branches, it will exude a sap that is used to soothe the pain of burns, rashes, insect bites, and other skin irritations. The aloe gel helps to speed the process of healing.

Please break off one of the branches.

Patient breaks off branch of the aloe plant. If they are unable to do so, break it off for them and lay it in front of them.

May God give you strength to claim new possibilities and gifts for your body, to stay active, to live and thrive. May God give you the enthusiasm to live passionately, to laugh, to love, to dream. Just as this aloe plant, though wounded, still provides healing balm, may God grant you healing as a resource for yourself and others, to show kindness and do good.

While giving this blessing, take some of the gel from the broken aloe branch and make the sign of the cross on the forehead of the patient.

________________ [patient name], receive this promise from God in 1 Peter (5:7, 10–11): "Cast all your anxiety on him, because he cares for you....The God of all grace, who has called you to his eternal glory in Christ will himself restore, support, strengthen and establish you. To Him be the power for ever and ever. Amen."

[If appropriate, make the sign of the cross together.]

Blow out candle, close notebook. Sit quietly with patient to see what further thoughts or reactions they might want to express or process.

STAFF RITUAL OF REMEMBRANCE, GRIEF, AND THANKSGIVING

GATHERING

This ritual began during COVID, as staff mourned the many traumas and losses they were undergoing. But it also has use for any group trauma or grief process. We limited the size of each group to eight people. We were limited by the half-hour time frame (which was all the time that staff could spare) and wanted to make sure that everyone got a chance to share if they wanted to.

Room Prep: Quiet music. Low lights. Table set with river stones and lighted candles. River stones have words like Strength, Joy, Peace, Wisdom, Courage, Hope, *and* Faith *written in gold or silver ink. Stones are turned face down. Chairs are in a circle, appropriately distanced. As people enter the room, they pick up a small votive candle and program card.*

Leader: Thank you for coming together for this half hour. We are here to remember with intention the losses, the traumas, and the layers of change that have occurred in this past year. There have been losses related to death and dying of staff members and their loved ones, loss of physical, mental, and spiritual well-being, and loss of community and more. The traumas associated with racial injustice have regurgitated and intensified. We have witnessed and lived through pain and suffering incurred by racial supremacy while being challenged to reflect on how our own attitudes and sources of power improve/hinder the lives of our neighbors, friends, and families.

The "normalcy," if there ever was such a thing, is gone. Many of the changes in this year have been unwelcome, difficult to understand, and full of unknowns. Our sense of community has completely broken down, and isolation, enforced to keep us safe, has caused disorientation, loss of connection, and the emergence of emotions like fear, anger, grief, and sadness. The pandemic has even upended our sense of time. You have your own concerns and stressors you bring with you today.

The first steps for healing from trauma are putting words to your story, "bearing witness," naming the losses, the learnings, the experiences, and secondly, telling your story to others...a community...in this case of your peers. We honor one another by sitting in silence as one person at a time shares a way in which they have been impacted.

After you speak, light your candle and place it on the center table. If you do not want to share in words, sit in silence and light the candle you hold.

TELLING

Twenty minutes of sharing by team members.

TAKING ACTION

After each person shares, they light their candle and put it on the table in the middle. The group listens to one another in respectful silence until everyone has had a chance to speak.

Leader: Thank you all for sharing. What did you realize as you listened to others? Is there anything you understand now that you didn't before?

You have observed that as you shared your stories, the light increased. Light has great significance for us, doesn't it? Light is one of the most universal and fundamental symbols for all people. It is illumination and intelligence. It stimulates sight and makes things visible, enables us to find our way. It is a sign of the divine, a source of goodness, ultimate reality, and strength that surrounds us.

You also picked up a rock. These are river rocks, worn smooth by the passage of water, in season and out of season, enduring the honing and abrasion that have made them beautiful today. You will find connections as you think about your own stories.

SENDING

I invite you to read together the following affirmations in your program:

- We acknowledge days and nights filled with anxiety as we work toward healing in healthcare.
- We acknowledge the strength needed for the continued pressure of isolation and loneliness at home and at work.
- We acknowledge our need for community, with its interaction of compassion, love, and hope, newly appreciated in our experience of loss.
- We give thanks for the compassionate care and selfless courage of our teammates.
- We give thanks for science of medicine which has protected us.
- We give thanks for _____________ [Allow for participants to offer their suggestions of thanks.]

Leader: Thank you for your participation. Please take your stone with you. The word on the other side is for you. Hope and light are ahead. Look for them! May you and your work be blessed. Amen.

GRATEFULNESS[144]

Chapters 5 and 6: "Engaging Power" and "Learning to Dream"

Let's start by focusing on your breathing. Breathe in and out several times...allowing the breath to come deeper and deeper... gently allowing yourself to turn your attention inward...interested in your own well-being...looking to see how you are for just this moment...allowing any worries or concerns you may have... to drift through your mind and out with your breath...letting your breath clear your mind as you begin to relax.

[Take about three to five minutes for this next part.]

Think about three people in your life you are grateful for [could be family, friends, someone in your past, even someone in history, someone who has spoken into your life]....While breathing slowly and deeply, bring the first person's face in front of your closed eyes. Try to "see" this person as clearly as you can. Remember the ways this person has contributed to your life. Then send him or her silent gratitude while continuing to breathe slowly and deeply. Repeat with the next person...and the next...and the next....Relish the few moments you spend remembering them. Say thank you to them.

Let yourself out of this deep state of relaxation gradually... knowing you can come back to it. Whenever you are ready to return to this day, reawaken your body slowly...gently moving your muscles...rolling your shoulders slowly forward...then slowly backward...leaning your head gently to the left...leaning your head gently to the right...wiggling your fingers and your toes....

Pause five seconds.

Whenever you are ready...

take a deep breath...

And open your eyes, taking a sense of gratefulness with you for your day.

PASSIVE PROGRESSIVE RELAXATION

Take a deep breath...now another....Do a quick body scan to see where you might be holding your stress...in your shoulders? In your back? In your jaw? In your tummy? See if you can let go of all you've been carrying today....Set it aside for a few moments... taking another deep breath...listening to where your body might be tight or tense or sore....And now...starting with the top of your head, feel relaxation beginning to spread downward...feeling your ears relax, your jaw relax, breathing deeply...and now spreading that relaxation to your neck and shoulders...and now down your back...breathing deeply...feeling relaxation spreading to your upper arms...your lower arms...your hands...your fingers...and now paying attention to your tummy and your abdomen...feeling relaxation spreading here, continuing to let go of whatever stress you might be holding. And now paying attention to your hips...your thighs...your knees...your shins...breathe...breathe... holding this relaxation...and now your feet...wiggle your toes... feeling the relaxation throughout your whole body...holding this for just a minute...continuing to breathe deeply. And now...rubbing your hands together, putting one hand on your heart and the other on your tummy. Feel the warmth of your hands, welcoming relaxation, letting go of stress. Say, "May I be kind to myself?" "May I find the strength and wisdom I need for today? Breathe... breathe....And now, shrugging your shoulders, tilting your head to the left, and to the right, stretching your arms and your legs... and when you are ready, opening your eyes, feeling relaxed and refreshed.

GUIDED IMAGERY: FAVORITE PLACE

Use a slow, even, almost monotone speech. Background music will enhance the experience.

Find a comfortable position. Lay your hands at your sides or on your lap, palms up. Close your eyes if you wish. Take a deep breath, all the way down to your diaphragm, holding it for a moment, and breathe it out. Again…deep breath in…and breathe out. Breathe in as deeply as is comfortable for you…letting go of any tension you might be holding….Continue breathing slowly and gently.…

As you become more relaxed, think of a favorite place.…It could be a vacation spot, the mountains, the seashore, a forest…it could be a room at home…whatever comes to your mind, sit with that a moment. Still breathing deeply, try to picture this place. Notice the details, the aromas, the colors, the sounds. What time of day is it? What season is it? Is there a warm sun? A cool breeze? Find a place to sit, open to all the details of your favorite place. How does it feel to be here? Do you feel safe? Secure? Happy? Restful? Continue to take deep, slow breaths, becoming more relaxed as you settle into your space. What memories come up for you as you sit in your favorite place? Just sit quietly, taking in the goodness of this place, breathing deeply, feeling grateful to be here. [*Spend a few minutes in silence.*]

When you are ready to return to this day, reawaken your body slowly…gently move your muscles…roll your shoulders slowly forward…then slowly backward…lean your head gently to the left…return to center…lean your head gently to the right… turn your head…

Wiggle your fingers and toes…stretch…gently open your eyes…feeling alert…calm…and full of energy. [*You might ask the patient to tell you about their experience.*]

BREATH PRAYER

This form of contemplative prayer is linked to the rhythms of breathing. Repeat a phrase over and over, timing it to your breathing. You might use: "Jesus, have mercy." As you inhale, pray: "Jesus." As you exhale, pray: "Have mercy." Other examples: "Show me…your way"; "Heal…me"; "Have…mercy"; "Guide…me."

This is very helpful in very stressful situations when breath and words are hard to come by.

DAILY EXAMEN

Adapted from a technique described by Ignatius Loyola in his Spiritual Exercises. https://www.ignatianspirituality.com/ignatian-prayer/the-examen/

It's time to review your day, or your week, or your experience. Take some deep breaths. Invite God's Spirit to come and show you what you need to see, hear, understand...

1. Become aware of God's presence.
2. Review the day with gratitude.
3. Pay attention to your emotions.
4. Choose one feature of the day, and pray from it.
5. Look toward tomorrow.

LECTIO DIVINA

Psalm 63

1 O God, you are my God, I seek you,
  my soul thirsts for you;
my flesh faints for you,
  as in a dry and weary land where there is no water.
2 So I have looked upon you in the sanctuary,
  beholding your power and glory.
3 Because your steadfast love is better than life,
  my lips will praise you.
4 So I will bless you as long as I live;
  I will lift up my hands and call on your name.
5 My soul is satisfied as with a rich feast,
  and my mouth praises you with joyful lips

6 when I think of you on my bed,
   and meditate on you in the watches of the night;
7 for you have been my help,
   and in the shadow of your wings I sing for joy.
8 My soul clings to you;
   your right hand upholds me.

FIRST READING: WHAT STANDS OUT?

Read the verses slowly and meditatively. Think about what it might feel like to be thirsty and weak. Where could you go for sanctuary?

SECOND READING: HOW DOES IT CONNECT WITH YOUR LIFE?

Why does this stand out to me? Is there a connection to my life?

THIRD READING: IS THERE SOMETHING NEW TO UNDERSTAND, OR THINK, OR DO?

Talk to God about what is coming up for you. What does this mean to you? How are you changed by this?

PRAYER
Give thanks for the chance to listen and talk with God
   through this passage. What do you take with you?

"THE GUEST HOUSE" BY RUMI[145]

Start by centering yourself and taking some deep breaths. Read through this slowly, and think about what's new for today, what needs to clear out, what you are grateful for...be open to what thoughts come.

This being human is a guest house.
Every morning a new arrival.
A joy, a depression, a meanness,
some momentary awareness comes
as an unexpected visitor.
Welcome and entertain them all!
Even if they are a crowd of sorrows,
who violently sweep your house
empty of its furniture,
still, treat each guest honorably.
He may be clearing you out
for some new delight.
The dark thought, the shame, the malice.
meet them at the door laughing and invite them in.
Be grateful for whatever comes.
because each has been sent
as a guide from beyond.

Rumi (thirteenth-century poet, Islamic scholar, theologian, and Sufi mystic from whom we have much wisdom)

EXPECTATIONS BY ABRAHAM JOSHUA HESCHEL

Think about the questions raised in this passage. What are you being called to? What are you waiting on? What is waiting on you?

Over and above personal problems, there is an objective challenge to overcome inequity, injustice, helplessness, suffering, carelessness, oppression. Over and above the din of desires there is a calling, a demanding, a waiting, an expectation. There is a question that follows me wherever I turn. What is expected of me? What is demanded of me? What we encounter is not only flowers and stars, mountains and walls. Over and above all things is a sublime expectation, a waiting for. With every child born a new expectation enters the world. This is the most important experience in the life of every human being: something is asked of me. Every human being has had a moment in which he sensed a mysterious waiting for him. Meaning is found in responding to the demand, meaning is found in sensing the demand.[146]

Abraham Heschel (Jewish theologian and philosopher, noted for his presentation of the prophetic and mystical aspects of Judaism and another wonderful source of wisdom)

BEING LOVED[147]

Consider God's gifts to me. God creates me out of love and asks nothing more than a return of love on my part. So much does God love me that even though I turn away and make little response, this Giver of all good gifts continues to be my Savior and Redeemer. (Ignatius of Loyola, Spiritual Exercises 234)

I have loved you with an everlasting love;
therefore, I have continued my faithfulness to you.
(Jer 31:3)

What are memories of being loved and cared for through my life? Being loved is an invitation to conversion and transformation. What happens inside me when I try to image a God who is crazy and passionate about me?

What aspect of the created world reminds me of God's care for all humankind?

How does the gift of being loved by God and others have a spill-over effect on every area of my life?

Notice what happens to my own desire to love as I become more aware of God's lavish care for me.

STRUGGLING WITH THE "WHY?" QUESTION[148]

We all ask "why?" when our lives go in a direction we didn't plan, or when trauma hits. Sometimes just sitting with our questions and knowing that we all ask this sometime in our lives can be helpful.

Why me? Why did God allow this? Why are my plans always frustrated? Why? Why didn't you stop this? Why don't you cure me? Why? Where are you? How long?

O Lord, how long shall I cry for help,
 and you will not listen?
Or cry to you "Violence!"
 and you will not save?
Why do you make me see wrongdoing
 and look at trouble?
Destruction and violence are before me;
 strife and contention arise. (Hab 1:2–3)

Even though...

Though the fig tree does not blossom,
 and no fruit is on the vines;
though the produce of the olive fails,
 and the fields yield no food;
though the flock is cut off from the fold,
 and there is no herd in the stalls,

yet I will rejoice in the LORD;
I will exult in the God of my salvation.
God, the Lord, is my strength;
he makes my feet like the feet of a deer,
and makes me tread upon the heights. (Hab 3:17–19)

You are enough.

"Lord, even if I lose my life in this holocaust, not just my goods, not just my home, not just my job, not my family, Lord, if I am destroyed I still put my faith in you, the God of my salvation. If everything as I know it here, including life itself, is snuffed out, Lord, you've promised to make my feet like the deer's feet and take me to the high place of heaven itself."

Paraphrasing Habakkuk's testimony from the sermon,
"O God, Why Me?" by Dr. Wilson Benton

PRAYER OF ADORATION

Psalm 71 and 72

In you, O LORD, I take refuge....
But I will hope continually,
and will praise you yet more and more....
Your power and your righteousness, O God,
reach the high heavens
You who have done great things,
O God, who is like you?
You who have made me see many troubles and
calamities
will revive me again;
From the depths of the earth
you will bring me up again.
You will increase my honor,
and comfort me once again....

Blessed be the LORD, the God of Israel,
who alone does wondrous things.
Blessed be his glorious name forever;
may his glory fill the whole earth.
Amen and Amen. (Pss 71:1, 14, 18–21; 72:18–19)

IDENTITY AND PURPOSE[149]

1 Kgs 19:11–13

[An angel] said "Go out and stand on the mountain before the LORD, for the LORD is about to pass by." Now there was a great wind, so strong that it was splitting mountains and breaking rocks in pieces before the LORD, but the LORD was not in the wind; and after the wind an earthquake, but the LORD was not in the earthquake; and after the earthquake a fire, but the LORD was not in the fire; and after the fire a sound of sheer silence. When Elijah heard it, he wrapped his face in his mantle and went out and stood at the entrance of the cave. Then there came a voice to him that said, "What are you doing here, Elijah?"

WHICH PART OF YOUR LIFE makes the most noise?

REFLECT FOR A FEW MINUTES on the sound of sheer silence, or "a still, small voice." What would that be like for you?

REFLECT ON GOD'S QUESTION to Elijah.

"Why are you here, Elijah?" Does not God know the reason for Elijah's presence? What is the purpose of the questions?

IF YOU WOULD BE ASKED that question today, "Why are you here?" What would be your answer?

CHOOSING LIFE

Deut. 30:19–20 *Moses talking to his people*

I have set before you life and death, blessings and curses. Choose life so that you and your descendants may live, loving the LORD your God, obeying him, and holding fast to him; for that means life to you and length of days, so that you may live.

Consider the choices you are making in your life.

Are my choices life-giving or made from fear, anger, or shame?

Are they consistent with my priorities and my goals for my life?

What am I holding on to that I could let go of?

LABYRINTH[150]

Print out a labyrinth from the internet. The subject can use a pencil or their finger as they process the path. Or, if you have access to a real labyrinth, take your group there. It can be a wonderful, interactive, sharing experience.

REMEMBER

Before walking the labyrinth, take time in gratitude to be thankful.

Bless the people in your life.

If there is a particular event or situation troubling you, bring it to mind and form a healing question around it.

RELEASE

Walking into the labyrinth.

This is the time to quiet the mind, let go of the mind chatter and release our troubles and distractions.

Open your heart to feel whatever it may feel.
Become aware of your breathing.
Take slow deep breaths.
Relax and move at the pace your body wants to go.
RECEIVE
Standing or sitting in the center.
This is a place of reflection, meditation, and prayer.
Pause and stay as long as you like.
Listen to the Spirit through your inner voice.
In the safety of this space, be receptive.
RETURN
Walking out of the labyrinth.
Begin walking out the same path you followed in.
As you walk out, integration of your experience happens.
Experience whatever healing, peace or sense of well-being may come.[151]

GOD OF COMFORT

Blessed be the God and Father of our Lord Jesus Christ, the Father of mercies and the God of all consolation, who consoles us in all our affliction, so that we may be able to console those who are in any affliction with the consolation with which we ourselves are consoled by God. For just as the sufferings of Christ are abundant for us, so also our consolation is abundant through Christ. If we are being afflicted, it is for your consolation and salvation; if we are being consoled, it is for your consolation, which you experience when you patiently endure the same sufferings that we are also suffering. Our hope for you is unshaken; for we know that as you share in our sufferings, so also you share in our consolation. (2 Cor 1:3–7)

WORRY

That is why I tell you not to worry about everyday life—whether you have enough food and drink, or enough clothes to wear. Isn't life more than food, and your body more than clothing? Look at the birds. They don't plant or harvest or store food in barns, for your heavenly Father feeds them. And aren't you far more valuable to him than they are? Can all your worries add a single moment to your life?

And why worry about your clothing? Look at the lilies of the field and how they grow. They don't work or make their clothing, yet Solomon in all his glory was not dressed as beautifully as they are. And if God cares so wonderfully for wildflowers that are here today and thrown into the fire tomorrow, he will certainly care for you. Why do you have so little faith?

So don't worry about these things, saying, "What will we eat? What will we drink? What will we wear?" These things dominate the thoughts of unbelievers, but your heavenly Father already knows all your needs. Seek the Kingdom of God above all else, and live righteously, and he will give you everything you need.

So don't worry about tomorrow, for tomorrow will bring its own worries. Today's trouble is enough for today. (Matt 6:25–34 NLT)

GUIDED IMAGERY: PROCESSING FEAR[151]

Matt 14:22–33

Imagine yourself in this story. Feel the sights, sounds, smells, and emotions that are at work.

Immediately he made the disciples get into the boat and go on ahead to the other side, while he dismissed the crowds. And after he had dismissed the crowds, he went up the mountain by himself to pray. When evening came, he was there alone, but by this time the boat, battered by the waves, was far from the land, for the wind was against them. And early in the morning he came walking toward them on the sea. But when the disciples saw him walking on the sea, they were terrified, saying, "It is a ghost!" And they cried out in fear. But immediately Jesus spoke to them and said, "Take heart, it is I; do not be afraid."

Peter answered him, "Lord, if it is you, command me to come to you on the water." He said, "Come." So Peter got out of the boat, started walking on the water, and came toward Jesus. But when he noticed the strong wind, he became frightened, and beginning to sink, he cried out, "Lord, save me!" Jesus immediately reached out his hand and caught him, saying to him, "You of little faith, why did you doubt?" When they got into the boat, the wind ceased. And those in the boat worshiped him, saying, "Truly you are the Son of God."

Reflections:

What was Peter thinking and feeling when he made his wild request? When he heard Jesus call him to come? When he actually took that first step onto the water? When he began to sink? When he cried out to Jesus? When he got back into the boat? What are your impressions of the sights, sounds smells, thoughts, and emotions of that scene?

Where were you in this story?

What came up for you?

What is the name of the fear that has the power to cause you to sink?

What act of faith might Jesus be calling you to undertake?

BETWEEN A ROCK AND A HARD PLACE

Isa 43:1–8

Put your name in this passage. God is speaking to *you*.

But now thus says the LORD,
he who created you, ________ [patient's name]
he who formed you, ________ [patient's name]

Do not fear, for I have redeemed you;
I have called you by name, you are mine.
When you pass through the waters, I will be with you;
and through the rivers, they shall not overwhelm you;
when you walk through fire you shall not be burned,
and the flame shall not consume you.
For I am the LORD your God,
the Holy One of Israel, your Savior....
Because you are precious in my sight,
and honored, and I love you...
do not fear, for I am with you.

REST

Ps 46:10

Be still, and know that I am God.

Introduce deep breathing...read through the psalm. Then drop off a word each time with thirty seconds of silence between:

Be still, and know that *I am God.*
Be still, and know that *I am.*
Be still, and *know*
Be *still*
Be...

GOAL SETTING

This is often helpful when hope arrives and one can begin to plan for a future. Goals should be specific, measurable, achievable, realistic, timely....

What is my goal?
What might be the roadblocks?
What will be the steps?

How will I know that I have completed this goal?
How will it benefit me?
Who will support and encourage me?

A SHORT GUIDE TO USING PSALMS

THANKSGIVING

9 "I will give thanks to the LORD with my whole heart; I will tell of all your wonderful deeds."
30:8–12 "You have turned my mourning into dancing."
136 "O, give thanks to the LORD...."

HOPE

33:20–22 "Let your steadfast love, O LORD, be upon us, even as we hope in you."
130 "I wait for the LORD, my soul waits, and in his word I hope."

FORGIVENESS

32 "Happy are those whose transgression is forgiven, whose sins are covered."
103:10 "He does not deal with us according to our sins...."

FAITHFULNESS

25 "Make me to know your ways."
37 "Take delight in the LORD, and he will give you the desires of your heart."
121 "I lift up my eyes to the hills—from where will my help come?"
139:13 "LORD, you have searched me and known me...it was you who formed my inward parts."

PRAISE

18 "The LORD is my rock...."
40 "He put a new song in my mouth...."
46:10 "Be still and know that I am God!"
57:5 "Be exalted, O God, above the heavens. Let your glory be over all the earth."
59:16 "But I will sing of your might; I will sing aloud of your steadfast love in the morning...."
66:5 "Make a joyful noise to God, all the earth...come and see what God has done."
84:10 "For a day in your courts is better than a thousand elsewhere."
89 "I will sing of your steadfast love, O LORD, forever."
95 "Let us come into his presence with thanksgiving...."
100:3 "Know that the LORD is God. It is he that made us and we are his."
145 "I will extol you, my God and King and bless your name...."
146 "I will praise the LORD as long as I live."
150 "Praise God in his sanctuary; Praise him in his mighty firmament."

CONFESSION

38 "Do not forsake me, O LORD; O my God, do not be far from me; make haste to help me, O LORD, my salvation."
51:10 "Create in me a clean heart."

SUFFERING, THIRST

6 "I am weary with my moaning."
13 "How long O LORD?"
22 "My God, my God, why have you forsaken me?"
31 "Be gracious to me, O LORD, for I am in distress."
42 "As a deer longs for flowing streams...."

55:4 "My heart is in anguish within me."
63 "O God, you are my God, I seek you, my soul thirsts for you."
77 "I cry aloud to God, aloud to God."

PROTECTION

3:3–4 "But you, O LORD, are a shield around me...."
16:9–11 "Protect me, O God, for in you I take refuge...."
20 "The LORD answer you in the day of trouble!"
23 "The LORD is my shepherd...."
27 "The LORD is my light and my salvation."
28 "To you, O LORD, I call; my rock...."
61:2 "Lead me to the rock that is higher than I...."
91:2 "My refuge and my fortress; my God, in whom I trust."

CREATION

8 "O LORD, how majestic is your name in all the earth!"
19 "The heavens are telling the glory of God...."
22 "The earth is the LORD's...."
104 "You set the earth on its foundations...."

PSALMS BY CATEGORY

Affliction: 27, 25, 40, 42
Alienation: 51
Asking for strength: 12, 30
Blessing of righteousness: 4, 5, 26, 37
Communal lament: 74, 79, 88 (dark night of the soul), 137
Complaint, need, submission: 143
Confession: 32, 38, 51
Creation: 19, 24, 121
Cry from the depths: 22, 130

NOTES

1. Ronald Rolheiser, *The Holy Longing* (New York: Doubleday, 1999), 7.

2. Jim Rendon, *Upside: The New Science of Post-Traumatic Growth* (New York: Touchstone, 2015), 9.

3. Rendon, *Upside*, 15.

4. Rendon, *Upside*, 15.

5. Rendon, *Upside*, 17.

6. Rendon, *Upside*, 97.

7. Viktor E. Frankl, *Man's Search for Meaning* (New York: Simon & Schuster, 1963), 76.

8. Frankl, *Man's Search for Meaning*, 147.

9. A. H. Maslow, *Motivation and Personality*, 2nd ed. (New York: Harper & Row, 1970), 150.

10. A. H. Maslow, *Toward a Psychology of Being*, 2nd ed. (New York: Van Nostrand, 1968).

11. Christopher Peterson and Martin E. P. Seligman, *Character Strengths and Virtues* (New York: Oxford University Press, 2004).

12. F J. Shih, S. S. Wang, S. M. Hsiao, P. H. Tseng, and S. S. Chu, "Comparison of Psychospiritual Needs of Chinese Heart Transplant Recipients at Pre- and Postoperative Stages," *Transplantation Proceedings* 40 (2008): 2597–99.

13. David R. Hodge, and Violet E. Horvath, "Spiritual Needs in Health Care Settings: A Qualitative Meta-synthesis of Clients' Perspectives," *Social Work* 56, no. 4 (2011): 306–16.

14. Term coined by Paul Ricoeur, twentieth-century French philosopher.

15. Bessel van der Kolk, *The Body Keeps the Score* (New York: Penguin, 2015), 81, emphasis added.

16. Jerome Groopman, *The Anatomy of Hope* (New York: Random House, 2004), 194.

17. Agustin Fuentes, *The Creative Spark: How Imagination Made Humans Exceptional* (New York: Penguin Publishing Group, 2017).

18. Peter A. Levine, PhD, *Healing Trauma* (2005; Boulder, CO: Sounds True, 2008), 9.

19. Miriam Akhtar, *What Is Post-Traumatic Growth?* (London: Watkins Publishing, 2017), 23.

20. van der Kolk, *The Body Keeps the Score*, 55.

21. Arthur W. Frank, *The Wounded Storyteller* (Chicago: University of Chicago Press, 1995), 60.

22. Peter A. Levine, *In an Unspoken Voice* (Berkeley, CA: North Atlantic Books, 2010), 31.

23. Rendon, *Upside*, 71.

24. Annie Dillard, *Teaching a Stone to Talk: Expeditions and Encounters* (New York: Harper Perennial, 1992).

25. Kenneth R. Mitchell and Herbert Anderson, *All Our Losses, All our Griefs* (Philadelphia: Westminster Press, 1983), 37.

26. Robert Grant, PhD, *The Way of the Wound* (Oakland, CA: Robert Grant, 1996), 237.

27. Wade Mullins (@wad3mullen), "Life can be shattered in a single moment...," Twitter, March 8, 2019.

28. Frederick Buechner, *Telling Secrets* (New York: HarperOne, 2000), 30.

29. Frank, *The Wounded Storyteller*, 53.

30. J. Harrold Ellens, "Sailing Close to the Wind," in *Flourishing in Faith: Theology Encountering Positive Psychology*, ed. Gillies Ambler, Matthew P. Anstey, Theo D. McCall, and Mathew A. White (Eugene, OR: Cascade Books, 2017), 132–33.

31. Madeleine L'Engle, *Walking on Water* (New York: Convergent, 2016), 37.

32. L'Engle, *Walking on Water*, 132.

33. van der Kolk, *The Body Keeps the Score*, 193.

34. Frank, *Wounded Storyteller*, 77.

35. Frank, *Wounded Storyteller*, 80.

36. Frank, *Wounded Storyteller*, 96.

37. Frank, *Wounded Storyteller*, 97.

38. Frank, *Wounded Storyteller*, 98.

39. Frank, *Wounded Storyteller*, 114.

40. Martin Buber, *Ten Rungs: Collected Hasidic Sayings* (New York: Routledge, 2020), 84.

41. Rendon, *Upside*, 75.

42. Miriam Greenspan, *Healing through the Dark Emotions* (Boston: Shambhala, 2003), 20.

43. Frank, *Wounded Storyteller*, 136.

44. See "A Short Guide to Using the Psalms."

45. Elisabeth Kübler-Ross, *On Death and Dying* (New York: Scribner, 1974).

46. Robert A. Neimeyer, PhD, "Reconstructing Meaning in Bereavement: Summary of a Research Program," *Estudos de Psicologia* 28, no. 4 (Oct–Dec., 2011): 421–26.

47. Lucia Martincekova and John Klatt, "Mothers' Grief, Forgiveness, and Posttraumatic Growth after the Loss of a Child," *OMEGA—Journal of Death and Dying* 75, no. 3 (May 31, 2016): 1–18.

48. Desmond Tutu, *God Has a Dream: A Vision of Hope for Our Time* (London: Rider Publishing, 2005), 25.

49. Parker Palmer, *On the Brink of Everything: Grace, Gravity, and Getting Old* (Oakland, CA: Berrett-Koehler Publishers, 2018), loc. 1370 or 2874.

50. Wendell Berry, *The Long-Legged House* (Berkeley, CA: Counterpoint Publishing), 2012.

51. Martin Buber, *I and Thou* (New York: Touchstone, 1970), 62.

52. Judith L. Herman, MD, *Truth and Repair: How Trauma Survivors Envision Justice* (New York: Basic Books, 2023).

53. Enterprise Community Partners, "Centering Healing, Serving Community: Lessons from Chicago," Enterprise (blog), June 2, 2021, https://www.enterprisecommunity.org/blog/centering-healing-serving-community-lessons-chicago.

54. Herman, *Truth and Repair*, 4.

55. Arielle Schwartz, *The Post-Traumatic Growth Guidebook* (Eau Claire, WI: PESI, 2020), preface.

56. Greenspan, *Healing through the Dark Emotions*, 14.

57. Lynne Dale Halamish and Doron Hermoni, *The Weeping Willow* (New York: Oxford University Press, 2007), 443.

58. Halamish and Hermoni, *The Weeping Willow*, 445.

59. van der Kolk, *The Body Keeps the Score*, 81.

60. Rendon, *Upside*, 202.

61. Amy Florian, Loyola University course, "Grief, Illness, and Death," 2009.

62. Florian, "Grief, Illness, and Death."

63. Palmer, *On the Brink of Everything*, loc. 927.

64. Nicholas Wolterstorff, *Lament for a Son* (Grand Rapids, MI: Eerdmans, 1987), 34.

65. Amanda Gorman, *The Hill We Climb: An Inaugural Poem for the Country* (New York: Viking, 2021).

66. Jerome Groopman, *The Anatomy of Hope* (New York: Random House, 2004), 208.

67. Groopman, *The Anatomy of Hope*, 199.

68. Elizabeth Bernstein, "Finding Hope When Everything Else Feels Hopeless," *Wall Street Journal*, October 27, 2020.

69. Bernstein, "Finding Hope When Everything Else."

70. Groopman, *Anatomy of Hope*, 26.

71. Groopman, *Anatomy of Hope*, 193.

72. Groopman, *Anatomy of Hope*, 179.

73. Groopman, *Anatomy of Hope*, 177.

74. Groopman, *Anatomy of Hope*, 178–79.

75. Emil Brunner, *Eternal Hope* (n.p.: Andesite Press, 2015), 7.
76. Greenspan, *Healing through the Dark Emotions*, 173
77. Greenspan, *Healing through the Dark Emotions*, 199.
78. Greenspan, *Healing through the Dark Emotions*, 196.
79. Greenspan, *Healing through the Dark Emotions*, 120.
80. Greenspan, *Healing through the Dark Emotions*, 116.
81. Greenspan, *Healing through the Dark Emotions*, 125.
82. Greenspan, *Healing through the Dark Emotions*, 133.
83. Groopman, *Anatomy of Hope*, 26.
84. Groopman, *Anatomy of Hope*, 120.
85. Quoted in Tori Zuasner, *When Walls Become Doorways: Creativity and the Transforming Illness* (New York: Random House, 2006), 274. Christian Johann Heinrich Heine was a German-Jewish poet, journalist, essayist, and literary critic. He is best known outside of Germany for his early lyric poetry, which was set to music in the form of *Lieder* by composers such as Robert Schumann and Franz Schubert.
86. Rick Rubin, *The Creative Act: A Way of Being* (New York: Penguin Press, 2023), 1.
87. Rendon, *Upside*, 164.
88. William Bridges, *The Way of Transition* (Cambridge: Perseus Publishing, 2001), 38.
89. T. S. Eliot, quoted in William Bridges, *Transitions*, 2nd ed. (Cambridge, MA: Da Capo, 2004), 107.
90. Jeff Manion, *The Land Between* (Grand Rapids, MI: Zondervan, 2010), 21.
91. Margaret Silf, *The Other Side of Chaos* (Chicago: Loyola Press, 1999), 18.
92. Bridges, *Transitions*, 12.
93. Bridges, *The Way of Transition*, 144.
94. Sabina A. Spencer and John D. Adams, *Life Changes* (New York: Paraview, 2002), 35.
95. Spencer and Adams, *Life Changes,* 41.
96. Bridges, *Transitions*, 12.

97. Spencer and Adams, *Life Changes*, 49.

98. Bridges, *Transitions*, xiii.

99. Bridges, *Way of Transition*, 119.

100. Michael Card, *Scribbling in the Sand* (Downers Grove, IL: InterVarsity Press, 2002), 39.

101. David Benner, *Opening to God* (Downers Grove, IL: InterVarsity Press, 2010), 116.

102. Rendon, *Upside*, 161.

103. Marie J. C. Forgeard, "Perceiving Benefits after Adversity: The Relationship between Self-Reported Posttraumatic Growth and Creativity," *Psychology of Aesthetics, Creativity, and the Arts* 7, no. 3 (2013): 245–64.

104. Tobi Zausner, *When Walls Become Doorways: Creativity and the Transforming Illness* (New York:Harmony, 2007), 14.

105. Rendon, *Upside*, 166.

106. Martin Buber, *An Intimate Portrait* (New York: Viking Press, 1971), 56.

107. Spencer and Adams, *Life Changes*, 41.

108. Bridges, *Way of Transition*, 39.

109. Rendon, *Upside*, 234.

110. Frederick Buechner, "Follow Me" *The Magnificent Defeat* (New York: HarperOne, 1985).

111. Abraham Joshua Heschel, *Man Is Not Alone* (London: Farrar, Straus and Giroux, 1976), 165.

112. Madeleine L'Engle, *Walking on Water* (New York: Convergent, 1980), 12.

113. Rendon, *Upside*, 148.

114. Rendon, *Upside*, 152.

115. In 2009, palliative healthcare professionals from twenty-seven countries at an International Consensus Conference reached agreement on this definition of spirituality: spirituality is a dynamic and intrinsic aspect of humanity through which persons seek ultimate meaning, purpose, and transcendence and experience relationship to self, family, others, community, soci-

ety, nature, and the significant or sacred. Spirituality is expressed through beliefs, values, traditions, and practices.

116. Jessica Grose, "Opinion Today," *New York Times*, June 28, 2023.

117. Frederick Buechner, *Beyond Words: Daily Readings in the ABC's of Faith* (New York: HarperCollins, 2009), 109.

118. Shane Clifton, "Flourishing in a Broken Body," in Ambler et al., *Flourishing in Faith*, 167.

119. Richard Rohr, "In the End, a New Beginning," Center for Action and Contemplation, November 28, 2022.

120. NANDA Internacional, *Diagnósticos de enfermagem: definições e classificação, 2009-2011* (Porto Alegre: Artmed; 2010), 452.

121. H.O.P.E, F.I.C.A, George Fitchett's "7x7" Model for Spiritual Assessment, Four FACTs, and more.

122. Frances Bacon, *The Advancement of Learning*.

123. Garma C. C. Chang, *The Practice of Zen* (New York: Harper, the Perennial Library, 1970).

124. Brian McLaren, *Faith after Doubt: Why Your Beliefs Stopped Working and What to Do about It* (New York: St. Martins, 2021), xi.

125. Steven Spielberg, director, *Indiana Jones and the Last Crusade*, Paramount Pictures, 1989.

126. Liel Leibovitz "Pedaling to Heaven," Leibovitz at Large, *First Things*, August 2022.

127. Peter Marty, "Gratitude, Need, and Desire," *Christian Century*, January 27, 2021, 3.

128. Frederick Buechner, *A Crazy, Holy Grace: The Healing Power of Pain and Memory* (Grand Rapids, MI: Zondervan, 2017), 66.

129. L'Engle, *Walking on Water*, 12.

130. L'Engle, *Walking on Water*, 172.

131. Anne Sexton, *Letter to a Monk*.

132. Crystal L. Park, Joseph M. Currier, J. Irene Harris, and Jeanne M. Slattery, *Trauma, Meaning, and Spirituality* (Washington, DC: American Psychological Association, 2017), 151.

133. Gabriele Prati and Luca Pietrantoni, "Optimism, Social Support, and Coping Strategies as Factors Contributing to Posttraumatic Growth: A Meta-analysis," *Journal of Loss and Trauma* 14, no. 5 (2009): 364–88, http://dx.doi.org/10.1080/15325020902724271.

134. van der Kolk, *The Body Keeps the Score*, 210.

135. van der Kolk, *The Body Keeps the Score*, 38.

136. Rubem Alves, *Tomorrow's Child: Imagination, Creativity, and the Rebirth of Culture* (Eugene, OR: Wipf and Stock Publishers, 2011), 204.

137. Jacques Philippe, *Interior Freedom* (New York: Scepter Publishers, 2007), 107.

138. Solomon Schechter, *Studies in Judaism*, First Series (Whitefish, MT: Kessenger Publishing, 2010), 151.

139. L'Engle, *Walking on Water*, 189.

140. Henri J. M. Nouwen, *Bread for the Journey A Daybook of Wisdom and Faith* (New York: HarperCollins, 2006), 25.

141. The Tree of Life is a narrative therapy project, designed by Ncazelo Ncube (REPSSI) and David Denborough (Dulwich Centre Foundation) for young people.

142. James R. Zullo, PhD, clinical and consulting psychologist in Chicago, and associate graduate faculty at IPS, Loyola, Chicago, until 2004.

143. Morrow Cimbalo, "Psychology and Spirituality of Life Transitions," fall 2010, Loyola University. Circles of Support concept resourced from James Zullo, PhD.

144. Amit Sood, MD, *The Mayo Clinic Guide to Stress-Free Living* (Cambridge, MA: Da Capo Press, 2013), 90.

145. *The Essential Rumi*, "The Guest House," trans. Coleman Barks with Reynold Nicholson, J. J. Arberry, and John Moyne (New York: HarperOne, 2004), 109.

146. Abraham Joshua Heschel, *Who Is Man?* (Stanford, CA: Stanford University Press, 1965), 107.

147. Carol Ann Smith and Eugene F. Merz, *Moment by Moment: A Retreat in Everyday Life* (Notre Dame, IN: Ave Maria Press, 2000).

148. Wilson Benton Jr., "A Profound Answer to the Pressing Question, 'Why?,'" in *Be Still My Soul*, ed. Nancy Guthrie (Wheaton, IL: Crossway, 2010), 55.

149. Alice Fryling, *Seeking God Together* (Downers Grove, IL: InterVarsity Press, 2009), 142.

150. http://www.fourthchurch.org/worship/labyrinth.html.

151. Richard Peace, "The Courage of Faith," in *Contemplative Bible Reading* (Colorado Springs, CO: NavPress, 1998), 85.